THE ORCHESTRA

THE
ORCHESTRA

The Lives Behind the Music

DANNY DANZIGER

HarperCollins*Publishers*

HarperCollins*Publishers*
77–85 Fulham Palace Road,
Hammersmith, London W6 8JB

Published by HarperCollins*Publishers* 1995
1 3 5 7 9 8 6 4 2

A catalogue record for this book is
available from the British Library

ISBN 0 00 255241 8

Photoset in Linotron Bembo by
Rowland Phototypesetting Ltd
Bury St Edmunds, Suffolk

Printed in Great Britain by
HarperCollinsManufacturing Glasgow

For Shelley-Anne

Instruments

FIRST VIOLINS

Cathy Craig
Tina Gruenberg
Colin Harrison
Nicola Hurton
John Kitchen
Kathy Loynes
Leo Phillips
Robert Pool

SECOND VIOLINS

Dermot Crehan
Fiona Higham
Joseph Maher
Geoffrey Price
Joakim Svenheden

FRENCH HORN

Richard Bissill
Nicholas Busch
Gareth Mollison

VIOLA

Steve Broom
Tony Byrne
Miranda Davis
Robert Duncan
David Godsell
Julian Shaw
Josephine St Leon

LEADER

Joakim Svenheden

TROMBONE

Colin Busby
Peter Harvey

TRUMPET

Denis Curlett
Lawrie Evans
Anne McInerny

TUBA

Owen Slade

CELLO

Ron Calder
Santiago Carvalho
Roger Lunn
John Sharp
Bob Truman

FLUTE

Celia Chambers
Simon Channing

DOUBLE BASS

Geoffrey Downs
Kevin Rundell
Bryan Scott

vii

THE ORCHESTRA

PERCUSSION
Rachel Gledhill

HARP
Rachel Masters

TIMPANI
Russell Jordan

BASSOON
John Price

COR ANGLAIS
Joan Graham

PICCOLO
Sarah Newbold

OBOE
Angela Tennick

SAXOPHONE
Martin Robertson

CLARINET
Richard Hosford
Stephen Trier

GUITAR
Stephen Smith

★ ★ ★

CONDUCTOR
Franz Welser-Möst

STAGE MANAGER
Ken Graham

PERSONNEL MANAGER
John Cobb

MARKETING DIRECTOR
Judith Grahame

Preface

THIS BOOK COULD have been about any first-class orchestra and the people in it. The interviews could tell the stories of other first-rate musicians, and still reflect the same thoughts and hopes and dreams, the same love or hatred for their instruments, for the conductor or, indeed, for the musical life. But by chance, or fate, or luck, or however these things are decided, this is the tale of the London Philharmonic.

The London Philharmonic Orchestra was born on 7 October 1932, created by Sir Thomas Beecham from the best players in the country. Its debut at the Queen's Hall, London, brought the audience to its feet – some even standing on their seats to cheer. 'Nothing so electrifying has been heard in a London concert for years,' wrote Ernest Newman, a critic who was never easily impressed, in *The Times*. 'The tone was magnificent, the precision perfect, the reading a miracle of fire and beauty.'

Sixty years on, the LPO is based at the Royal Festival Hall, on the south bank of the Thames and, for three decades, it has been the resident orchestra at Glyndebourne in the summer months.

The LPO is a collection of people always striving for perfection in performances. To discover what is the personal price paid by a musician who has devoted himself or herself to learning their craft . . . read on.

THE ORCHESTRA

Richard Bissill
Co-principal French Horn

'Sometimes Gareth's doing something so funny I have
to play with my right eye closed, so my nose blocks
the sight of him . . .'

WE HAD A PIANO which my grandma gave us, it was in the
front room for ages, and I never used to touch it. One day, my
dad asked, 'Are you going to play this piano or not?' and I said,
'Probably not.' So we smashed it up, and took it down to the
tip – which is amazing, isn't it?

Shortly after that, there was a film on the television, Cornell
Wilde playing the part of Chopin, with all the melodrama of his
consumption, you know, blood dropping on the keys and so
on. I was bawling my eyes out watching this, and I said, 'Maybe
I wouldn't mind playing the piano after all . . .' And dad and
mum went out and got one on hire purchase.

When the music adviser for the county came around our school
looking for players he gave me a French horn, which I had to
share with another lad, and every night, my mum used to make
me disinfect the mouthpiece before giving it to him. Nevertheless, I began to love playing the horn, and completely forgot
about the piano at home.

Eight years ago, I applied for a job in the LPO. I came from
another London symphony orchestra, which was known to be
very hard and cynical. I couldn't believe how happy and friendly

it was here, people were saying, 'Hello, nice to see you.' People from the string section, God forbid, were actually speaking to me. This is a very happy bunch of people, with lots of good humour and jokes.

String musicians, particularly viola players, are generally the brunt of jokes in orchestras. They're made out to be a bit thick, and there are all sorts of jokes at their expense: What's the difference between a viola player and a Cornish pasty? A Cornish pasty is only 50 per cent vegetable. Or, a viola player goes into a shop and says, 'I'd like a copy of *The Strad*' – which is a magazine for string players. The shopkeeper says, 'You're a viola player aren't you?' and he says, 'Yes, how do you know?' 'This is a chip shop!' There are loads of them.

They take it all in good humour. I think they quite like to hear them.

I'm first French horn with Nick Busch, we're joint principals. First horns take a battering and we need to take it off our lips to give ourselves a rest before playing solos. Brass players can only do so much a day before they get tired. The instrument is tiring, especially if you're doing big hard blows, and there is a danger that your lips can get bruised and you then start abusing your face to get the note, and it ends up not sounding very good so you have what's called a 'bumper', who is there to give the first horn a rest basically. Nick and I bump each other up – which I admit is a strange expression.

I have a lot of respect for Nick. I know how difficult it is playing first horn and for him to have done it as long as he has is really fantastic. He plays some things really beautifully.

I think it's really important to enjoy yourself, there's no point sitting there poker-faced. Gareth, who's second horn, is a great mate, he and I have a good laugh. Sitting at the back of the orchestra, we're not under the conductor's nose, and we can get away with a certain amount of murder. Sometimes Gareth's doing something so funny, I have to play with my right eye closed, so my nose blocks the sight of him, because if brass

4

players get the giggles, their *embouchure* is all over the place and they just can't play.

I get a bit cross when things aren't going well and people make mistakes: I don't mean split notes or wrong notes, but people not playing in the right place, misreading rhythms, that sort of thing. I can feel myself getting tense and then I'll shout out some obscenity – and realize everyone has heard it and cower down behind my stand. But it's only because I want things to be good.

It's very easy to get cynical in any job but I try not to lose sight of the reason I started music in the first place, which was because I love it. I love it when I get what I call the tingle factor – which happens to me quite a lot, I'm glad to say.

There are always bits in the Strauss and Mahler, big romantic things, that get me going. And there's a lesser-known composer whom I've got a bee in my bonnet about, called Korngold. I love him. He's not highly regarded by classical snobs: he made a lot of money scoring all those Errol Flynn swashbuckling films. That romantic slushy stuff gets to me every time, even films like *ET* make me cry because of the music.

We, the horn section, have a bit of a battle with the percussion. Because percussion are right behind us, the shock waves are terrible: you get the cymbals or bass drums whacked behind you, the waves shoot right up your bell, and it gets you on the lips.

When we have big pieces, the whole back row is just percussion and there's hardly any point in playing. There is a piece called *The Pines of Rome* by Respighi, one of those Italian jobs. It is fantastic music actually – that's another tingle factor – except for the percussion. At the end of it, there is a big triumphant march when the centurions are marching into the city and all hell is let loose – the organ is blaring, percussion is knocking ten tons of shit out of everything – with all this noise coming back at you, it is absolute agony.

★　　★　　★

Music will always be my life, I can't imagine being without it really. The people I feel closest to and empathize with are musicians, most of my good friends are musicians. I'm not particularly interested in much else, and when I'm at home, if I'm not being forced into doing some decorating or something, I'll try and write some music.

It must be a bit infuriating at times for my wife, because musicians have their heads in the clouds, and my wife will be talking to me but I'm not really listening – that happens quite a lot, actually, and she gets quite annoyed.

Music is there all the time, and I love doing it. Long may it continue.

Steve Broom

Viola

'I was wondering whether Julian had had what we call
the "piss-off" letter'

I WAS BROUGHT UP in South Wales, a place called Pontypridd.
My family is quite religious, and we used to go to a Baptist
chapel called Bethlehem on a Sunday morning, so I suppose
singing hymns was my first idea of music.

Actually, I really wanted to play the French horn but there
weren't any school instruments for me to play. So the teacher
said, 'Come on, try the viola.' I did, and it seemed to suit me.
Because there were very few boys in the school who played the
viola, I was more involved than if I had just been one of the
violin players.

I have a wonderful instrument; I bought it at J & A Beare, which
is one of the most famous string-instrument shops in London,
they've been going well over a hundred years. My viola was
made in Edinburgh in 1853 by a Scottish viola maker, Thomas
Hardie who, it turns out, was a loose liver and inveterate drunk.
One day he got drunk and fell down the stairs and broke his
neck, which is how he died. But in his sober moments he made
exceptionally good instruments, including mine.

Sitting in the middle of any string section, there are obvious
frustrations, you feel your chance to blossom is pretty limited
sometimes. I have to bend what I'm doing to make it work with

the principal viola and, when you want to do it your way, it can become a bit frustrating.

I've just had an audition as principal viola at Covent Garden. Initially, there were forty of us. For my selection I played *Fantasie* by Hummel, who was a contemporary of Mozart, which seemed appropriate at an opera audition. I'm now through to the final round of auditions, down to the last eight players. We're playing the final audition in ten days' time.

Actually, my desk partner Julian Shaw applied for the job as well. Julian has quite a remarkable technique; his facility on the viola is exceptional. I mean, for his audition he played a piece by Paganini, which is the sort of thing virtuoso violin players play. He practises that sort of thing – although to my way of thinking that is rather pompous. I believe the viola is more a lyrical, singing instrument than a virtuoso instrument – and I think I make a better viola sound.

I was quite glad to get through to the next round, because players from the middle section who apply for a principal job might be thought to be jumping above themselves.

When I got the letter saying I was through to the second round, I was wondering whether Julian had had what we call the 'piss off' letter, because he was in a foul mood that day. I assumed he hadn't got through, but he had.

I think I will get through rather than Julian, but if it were to go the other way, it wouldn't be a huge surprise.

Colin Busby

Trombone

'One or two cheered'

THERE WERE LOTS of furniture factories in my home town, High Wycombe, and most of them had brass bands. When I was eight years old, I got into a top-class band called Ercolani's, and we played everything from *Poet and Peasant* right through to tunes from the Noël Coward shows. My job was to bang the cymbals but the trouble was, being small, everybody had bigger strides than me, and when I walked in the marching band, I was almost running.

The memories I have, they go way back, my wife is always amazed. I can remember the LPO coming to the town hall; I remember the programme as if it were yesterday. The first half was the *Swan Lake* Suite – I couldn't believe what a beautiful sound that was. In the second half, the 'Emperor' Concerto and the 'Pathétique' Symphony were really something too. And I realized, 'That's it, *that* is what I want to do.'

I can remember buying my first trombone. I went into Parker Studios in Soho and I thought, 'This is heaven.' There were lots of musicians hanging around, trying out the instruments, and one old man came up and showed me a trombone that was £75, which sounded like £7000 to me. 'We can give you a secondhand one,' they said. But, no, I wanted a new one. 'What about hire purchase, then?'

I selected a Besson, which is like the Rolls-Royce of

9

trombones. I loved the sound it made. The case was leather, a lovely tan colour, and the inside was blue velvet.

In the hands of the right person, the trombone is a super instrument. In the hands of a bad person, it's the laughable instrument that people have joked about for years. But it's a very versatile instrument. Brahms writes beautifully for the trombone; Shostakovitch uses it as an exciting, blaring instrument; Tchaikovsky writes very well for it; as does Mahler, of course.

You need very good breath control, because there's a lot of tubing to fill. I'm a little fellow, but I have a forty-two-inch chest, which has been developed over goodness knows how many years.

I went to the Liverpool Harmonic and became first trombone there. I was then invited to do an audition at the LPO on the recommendation of John Pritchard, the conductor. I got the job and I've been here thirty-one years, come the 15th of this month.

When I joined the LPO, the orchestra was striving for survival; we didn't sound very good and, for a very long time, we didn't have any commercial work at all. The brass section sound was awful, and one day the whole section was sacked, and only two of us were reinstated.

When Haitink came, things started to pick up. He was very introvert, a terribly shy man, he only came alive when he was on the box. But you respected everything he did, his tempos were always just right. The thing about great conductors is that they can raise you above yourself, they make you play much better than you normally play. There was a great empathy between him and the orchestra, and the audience loved him too. Wonderful new players came in, and we started to give fantastic concerts – every concert was a great occasion.

Life isn't all a bed of roses. Because we see more of each other than we do our wives, somewhere along the line we're going to fall out about something or other, especially on tour. Tours are murder for tempers, because people get overtired and conditions are often bad.

Once upon a time, we had a very small amount of women; now we have about a third, so dressing-room space is more cramped. They want all the privileges of a woman, and all the privileges of a man, at the same time. And they're the ones that smoke, hardly any of the men smoke.

I've worked very hard for the LPO, I've been very dedicated. I hardly take any time off, I've sat with pneumonia in one instance.

I consider thirty-one years to be a pretty good innings and so does everyone else – as I've often been reminded: 'Isn't it about time you went and did something else?' they say, and other hurtful comments.

I know what the attitude is these days, and not just in my business. I know people in other professions – my friends in the banks, for instance – who have been usurped because they've reached a particular age.

When I was celebrating my twenty-fifth year with the orchestra we were doing some recording sessions and John Cobb, the orchestra manager, got up and said, 'I'd just like to tell you, Colin Busby is celebrating his twenty-fifth anniversary in the orchestra.' One or two cheered. The break came and I walked over to the notice board to see if there were any alterations in the schedule. A girl, a young girl, who wasn't even a member of the orchestra, came up to me and said, 'Have you been in the orchestra for twenty-five years?' and I said, 'Yes'. 'Don't you think it's about time you retired,' she said, 'and gave somebody else a chance?' I was completely stunned by that.

Not everyone is like that, but I don't really want to have to combat that sort of attitude when I have so many other things I want to do. I especially want to be with my wife, Betty. She has cancer. I don't know how much longer she is going to live. She's doing magnificently at the moment and she could go on for twenty years – or she could die in three months.

Nicholas Busch
Co-principal French Horn

'Someone in the horn section had a nervous breakdown'

MY FATHER WAS A COMPOSER; he died when I was five. The French horn happened to be one of my father's favourite instruments, and my mother arranged for horn lessons.

Actually, I wanted to go to farming college. I was mad about farming. But I got a scholarship to the Royal College of Music and, being fairly lazy, I thought that might be easier. The LPO had a vacancy when someone in the horn section had a nervous breakdown, so I thought I might try for that.

You have to be mad to play the horn. I mean, it's twelve foot of brass with a small mouthpiece, and the distance between the notes is very small, and it's easy to hit a wrong note. So it's a tricky thing. It's generally reckoned to be the hardest instrument in the orchestra to play.

Also, because you can easily be heard, if your standards are not high enough they will get rid of you. It's not like being a rank-and-file fiddle player, who can sit there forever and never be heard, like a lot of them do, I'm afraid to say.

Wind and brass players tend to have rather a short life – the nerve goes, and most people end up not being able to play. Did you know, the Inland Revenue allows us to take our pensions at fifty-five?

In the pit, we are sat behind the woodwind and percussion, unfortunately. It's such a loud racket, very unpleasant. You get

13

a bass drum banging away near you, and you can feel the sound waves coming right up the bell on to your lip, which is a horrible sensation.

Of course, the majority of conductors are rubbish. Someone like George Solti is awful. I think he's the worst conductor ever – his style is just so undisciplined. I like Franz, I actually think he's good, although a lot of people don't, they are very disparaging of him. Tennstedt's good, but he's as mad as a hatter. I like him, but I've had many rows with him over the years. I respect Haitink, although he behaves very badly at times, like a spoilt child, but that's just him letting his private life override his conducting.

When people hear you're a musician, they usually ask, 'Gosh, do you go abroad a lot? How wonderful.' And I say, 'Well, it's not that marvellous, sitting on a bus in Germany for three weeks, one night stands all over the place.'

Generally speaking, touring is hard work. There are all those dreadful time differences, and you feel you've never slept properly. We go to Japan, and it's like being anywhere in the world, McDonald's everywhere. We did a tour last March: Tokyo, Los Angeles, Mexico City and New York – the four most polluted cities in the world.

I can never wait to get home. I have a farm now. It is only twenty-two acres but I'm not complaining, it's marvellous, and I work for the big landowner next door as a tractor driver in their busy periods.

I think about farming all the time, I love it. Even when I'm playing in the orchestra, I think about whether I should buy a new baler this year, or I think of the buildings I've got to repair, and the tractors I'd like to buy if I had the money.

To be honest, I'd like to retire from playing the horn. In fact, I would have liked to retire twenty years ago and done my farming. Of course, it was totally impossible, we have a family to bring up, and so I've had to stick at the horn.

But I've had enough of it. I've been playing professionally for thirty-three years now, and first horn all those years, and that's a long time. I feel I've done it all with orchestral playing. And I've always hated practising, I do the minimum to keep me in reasonable shape.

In the summer, when there are the light evenings, I have to practise immediately after breakfast, otherwise once I've gone out on to my land and played with my tractors, I forget about it, and by the time I come in, it's too late, and I don't feel like it.

Tony Byrne

Co-principal Viola

'A marvellous feeling of do or die . . .'

MY MOTHER GAVE ME my first instrument. I remember it very well, it was a cheap factory violin with a label inside, 'Copy of a Stradivarius'. I wish I had it now, out of nostalgia.

It was a tough background, tough in the sense that very often we didn't have a lot to eat, and we were very poorly dressed – I can remember getting up in the morning and thinking, 'gosh it's raining again, I'm going to have wet feet for the rest of the day.'

We were keen on music in the house. My mother was a singer, my elder brother was a jazz musician and another brother had a marvellous boy-soprano voice.

I didn't think I had any chance of making it in the musical profession, because coming from a poor family there was no opportunity to study at a college – we had no knowledge of grants or things like that – and I went to a Christian Brothers school, where they are not noted for their sensitivity for anything to do with the arts. However, in my spare time I was practising all I could on the violin, learning the repertoire studies, out of love, really, I was crazy about it.

I was given lessons from a lady who taught at the school where my sisters went, and she didn't take any fees. She was very generous. She said to me one day, 'You've started rather late, would you be interested in taking up the viola?'

17

I resisted this idea at first, because I had the notion that the viola was a second-class citizen compared to the violin. But, eventually, I got myself a viola, I bought it in a little shop off Ainger Street, from a man who was my namesake, and began to like it.

If the violin is like a soprano, the viola is much more contralto, and it's tuned in fifths, so it goes down a lower range. It has an amazingly dark, distinctive colour, and I have to say, I think the tonal range of the viola is wider than the violin, although the violin is perhaps more agile.

At this stage I was working for the Dublin Corporation – a dead end job but, honestly, I simply had to. I couldn't stay at school when my father died, because there was just no money in the house.

But my brother had joined a dance band, and he told me there was a vacancy coming up. I practised like crazy for about a month, and got the job.

We used to play seven nights a week at hotel dances at the Gresham Hotel, which is the big hotel on Connell Street, and I would get up early in the morning so I could practise all day. You would think the world of the dance band was very slipshod, very casual, but our band leader insisted on good time-keeping and proper appearance.

We played all the standards. I can even remember the numbers in the library pad: twenty-seven and twenty-eight were 'On The Street Where You Live' and 'I Could Have Danced All Night' – these things stick in your mind!

The guys in the band were very encouraging to me. One man kept saying, 'You will never know what the music profession is like unless you go to London.' I didn't really want to leave Dublin, I enjoyed the life there, but the problem with Dublin is you don't get big conductors, people like Haitink, Muti, Mehta, any of those . . . and I always wondered what it would be like. So I auditioned for the Hallé Orchestra, and I was accepted there. In fact, I played to Sir John Barbirolli! Can you imagine? I mean, to me he was a legend.

I remember the day I did the audition, the principal viola had got caught in a traffic jam, so I played just to Sir John. When the principal eventually arrived, Sir John said to him, 'Well, you can take it as read, we'll offer him a job.' I was so pleased, of course. But I was too young, and I couldn't get a union card.

Eventually, I moved to Bournemouth. I was principal viola in the Bournemouth Sinfonietta for seven years. It was a very pleasant life, and I loved living in Bournemouth, it's a gorgeous place. But I remember I used to say to my wife, 'I would be delighted to be exhausted by working', because I used to find the workload all too light. In a provincial town, you don't get that sense of a really important occasion which you get in a big orchestra. You'd open the Saturday papers and see all the concert announcements and foreign tours with the most outstanding conductors, and again, you'd think to yourself: 'Could I make it in London?'

One day I saw an advertisement in the paper for number four viola at the LPO, so I auditioned for that.

At the audition I played the Stamitz concerto, which is still considered one of the best audition pieces for viola. The viola doesn't have a great repertoire like the violin and the cello, they tend to be lesser known works. As a result, you find viola players are very interested in their literature, simply because you have to be a bit of a detective to find the best pieces. For example, if I would ask you about a cello concerto, I'm sure you would think of Elgar or Dvořák. If I said violin concertos, there are so many, Mozart alone wrote six, and you would think of Beethoven and Brahms too. But viola concertos – I bet you couldn't think of one.

Anyway, they must have liked what I played, because I got the job.

I remember the first concert I did, which was with Haitink. It was tremendous, we had never had conductors of that stature in Bournemouth, nor soloists like Rostropovich and Perlman – it was a wonderful thrill. It still is, I have to say.

I did find the repertoire extremely difficult. Before, I'd been playing Mozart, Schubert and Haydn, who are relatively simple for the viola parts. In the classical repertoire, the first violins carry the most difficult parts and the viola parts very often have repeated notes, which are not technically difficult to play. When the history of music moved forward, people like Berlioz, Wagner and Strauss started treating each section in virtuoso and soloistic ways, so the viola parts became much more difficult. So there was a lot of learning to be done, and I found it really taxing for the first year.

Obviously, the standard of the players makes an orchestra in the first place, but the one person who can galvanize things is the conductor: it's the force of his personality that will bring people along with him. Players might have played a symphony hundreds of times, so it takes quite a bit of doing for somebody to get them enthusiastic about it. That's why they are such larger-than-life characters.

They also get larger-than-life fees. Conductors can command incredibly big fees, but we have to try and get the best conductors because they ensure a better standard for the orchestra, and they also bring in a bigger crowd. But the fees are so enormous, and the players get so little by comparison, it seems to me that some of the major conductors are, in a way, bleeding it dry a bit . . .

The better the conductor, the more influential he is on sound colour. Take the Sibelius we performed the other night. That symphony is often done very slowly, but with Franz it had a headstrong charge which I found very exhilarating; I think Franz is almost reckless in these things, but it's a young man's prerogative, it's passionate music-making. Maybe when he's ten years down the road he'll do it differently.

One thing about musicians, when the chips are down, they are great ones for really pulling out that last ounce. I can remember a concert in Berlin with Klaus Tennstedt. Berlin is his home town and he was stoking us up into a frenzy of nervousness. Something went slightly wrong. In the beginning of Mahler 5, there is a transition where the music goes from four into two, and we misunderstood his beat somehow – I don't know how – and it was quite a panic. But there was this amazing feeling we must get together again, a marvellous feeling of do or die, and it was a very good concert.

What I like about this profession is that it's a meritocracy, pure and simple, it's a great leveller. We have public schoolboys, we have Irish, English, German, we have lots of different backgrounds and ideas, but we're all equal on that platform, and we all have a shared purpose – we want to send that audience out believing we're the best.

On tour, we socialize quite a lot. I often think touring brings an orchestra together. Sometimes we get very boisterous; Dermot, another Irishman on second violins, is a marvellous traditional fiddle player, and if it's a free day, and we're stuck on the coach, we'll enjoy a few beers and everyone gets a bit wild.

It's a great opportunity to be selfish for a bit, which is a great luxury, especially when you've got kids. I don't have to think of anybody but myself from the time I get up to the time I go to bed; I don't have a telephone to answer; I can practise in the day; and, if I'm in a town, I can go and see the sights – it's wonderful.

I am crazy about music. I listen to concerts in the evening, I put on the radio all the time, I think I probably drive my wife a bit mad.

I'd hate to lose the enthusiasm, because for me, it's not just a job. On a free day I'm very happy to do six hours' practice, because I actually like playing the instrument. I would hate it to become a job where I thought, 'Oh God, not another Beethoven 9'. That would be death. I don't think that will happen because sometimes I am on the platform with people of the most incredible stature, people like Barenboim and Zubin Mehta, who are so talented. Or take some of the instrumentalists like Rostropovich and Perlman, the technical ability of these people! And I think, I'm on the same platform, and I'm privileged to be here . . .

I love the job, yes, I love it.

Ron Calder
Cello

'The performance was never any good, and I had let
her down again'

YOU'RE ONLY AS GOOD as the last few notes you've played.

I don't wake up in the morning and think, 'God, I'm insecure.'
But, occasionally, you get on the Festival Hall platform and you
think, 'What am I doing here?' And there is a spiral you can go
through, that I did go through, very dramatically, about ten
years ago.

Having left the Scottish National Orchestra, where I was very
comfortable, I came down here, and, wowee, the best conductor
we ever got up there was someone who would be regarded as
very second rate by the London Philharmonic.

Bernard Haitink was the boss at the time. He was doing
Mahler symphonies, and it was like a wall of death.

Haitink is the greatest conductor I've ever worked with,
and ever will, but looking at him, and realizing that whatever
happened, he was doing it right and it was up to me to match
that . . . I panicked.

A colleague rescued me. I'd say to him, 'Tom, I can't sit on
the outside tonight,' and he would say, 'All right, I'll move
over,' and would cover for me. I could play at the heel end of
the bow, and I could play at the top end, but getting it from
one end to the other was downright impossible.

Also, my last wife was very, very critical. I was always

terrified when she came to watch me play. She would deliver the post-mortem on the train going back. It would start: 'Why didn't you invite me round to the back? I saw other wives going round the back.' Or, 'It didn't sound very good, did it?' The sort of things you don't really want to talk about.

But she couldn't know what the pressure of performing was like. Part of going to a live performance is seeing how the orchestra can achieve a performance as near perfect as it can get, but the fact that it's not perfect, one can take for granted. Only, she didn't.

In many ways, we were totally mismatched, my wife and I. This is terrible to say, but it was a disaster from the very beginning.

We met at university; we got together through playing chamber music. She used to play with her brother, who was a genius, the type of guy who plays Mendelssohn at two years old. They made an extremely good duo, and I really shouldn't have joined them, because I was never good enough.

She'd say to me, 'I told you not to do that,' and 'I told you not to hold that note so long,' or 'Why on earth did you do that?' No matter how well *I* thought I did, the performance was never any good, and I had let her down again.

She would always have the last word – she's a very good user of words – and I felt tied in knots, so I'd just walk away. We never even had a row.

I wanted to say that she didn't understand. But she did understand. It destroyed my self-respect as a cellist.

So why I married her, I don't know, but we stayed married for nineteen years, and had two kids.

The marriage ended because I met Perry, and we started making love. Eventually, I had to tell Muriel, and we sat down and talked about it. I was amazed how civilized it was, she was wonderful over it really. And she looks ten years younger now, so obviously it was getting to her too.

★   ★   ★

Having Perry sitting in the audience watching, and my friends in the orchestra seeing her and waving to her, well, I have a grin six feet wide knowing she is there – and is on my side.

I wouldn't be doing anything else, and I wouldn't be playing in any other orchestra. The sound we make together is magic – and the people I've had the chance of meeting and working with! Rostropovich playing Tchaikovsky, we've done a lot of work with Barenboim and Sir Adrian Bolt, and Haitink, of course. Maybe the fees for conductors are inflated, but the difference a good conductor makes is just incredible.

I'm really pleased to be where I am, I would say, dead lucky. If you like orchestral music, and you respect people like Beethoven, it's a wonderful life. I wouldn't have done anything else.

Santiago Carvalho
Cello

'I feel like a fish . . .'

I COME FROM a very beautiful city in Brazil. My father played the clarinet in a military band, and he taught me music theory and harmony. He was a good teacher, very patient, very inspiring. I am the eldest of seven brothers, and one girl, and we all played.

I entered a national competition in Brazil. The prize was a scholarship to study at the Academy of Music in London. I won, and I couldn't believe it. At that time, I was playing in night clubs in Rio de Janeiro and some very low, bad places, one or two brothels even. I had to do this to pay for my cello lessons. I had a very generous teacher. I paid him very little, considering he would give tuition for two or three hours. He had a beautiful flat opposite Copacobana Beach, oh boy, that was wonderful.

When I came here I couldn't speak English at all, and I apologize that my English still is not good.

Unfortunately, I have just had an accident. My daughter, poor girl, she closed the car door on my hand, caught the first finger of the left hand, so I haven't played in the orchestra for three months nearly. I went to see a consultant yesterday, and he said it could take months before this heals, because it's a fracture.

Well, I feel like a fish living out of water, because I love playing, I want to play, and I can't play. I can practise with fingers two, three and four, and I have had to invent some new exercises until I get better.

Every morning I listen to Antonio Negro, Haifitz and Bach. Music is my vitamin of life, it makes me feel good.

I miss everyone in the orchestra very much, my goodness, yes. When we get together, we make wonderful music. When something like this happens, I realize it is a blessing what I do. It is a very difficult profession, we work very hard to earn our living but, even so, I love playing in the orchestra. I think if you take up an instrument for a living, you must love it very much.

I spend so much time with the orchestra, sometimes I feel more married to the orchestra than my own wife. The orchestra does take over your life, and that is very dangerous for marriage, if one is not careful. For instance, we go on wonderful tours, stay at the best hotels, and after a concert, there's a wonderful feeling, especially when we've played well. And then you go out for dinner, and you miss home . . . and all the affairs begin, if one is not careful. It's very dangerous.

After all, music is romanticism, isn't it?

Celia Chambers
Co-principal Flute

'We exchanged glances over that, right there in the performance'

I WAS BESOTTED with sounds from an early age, anything I could get hold of that made some sort of noise, pitched or otherwise, and I started to play things like the harmonica, penny whistle and recorder.

Once every three weeks on a Saturday morning, the music mistress at our school took us on the train from Orpington to the Royal Festival Hall. That was my first introduction to music and an orchestra.

I would gaze down at the LSO, and there was Alex Mayer, the principal flute – oh, he was very handsome, carried himself very well – and if there was somebody playing in his place, I was a bit disappointed . . . and I thought, I want to play the flute, too.

One day my father came home with a flute. It was silver plate, very shiny, with a bright, scarlet, padded case. To me it was beautiful and, actually, I didn't make too bad a sound on it.

When I was fifteen, I joined the woodwind section of the Kent Youth Orchestra. When the coach looked at my flute, he said, 'Well, that's good to poke the fire with.' I was absolutely devastated that somebody could talk about my beautiful flute that way. *I* now coach the woodwind of the Kent Youth Orchestra, and I never ever tell anyone their flute is only good to poke the fire with, even if it is.

My mother died in my second year of music college and that completely knocked me for six. I didn't have a lot of friends, I was very quiet and shy, and I found the bereavement very hard to cope with. It took some months to get my act together. Then I said to myself, right, I have to channel my energies into playing the flute. I focused on performance, on playing, on what music meant to me, and I started to practise vehemently.

That was the beginning of a period when people noticed who I was and what I was doing, and I won prizes and I got a scholarship to go abroad.

A little later I got married, had two children, and was terribly busy being a mother. But I couldn't leave music alone; there was just no way the flute was going to be put in its box and forgotten. Every time the phone rang and there was freelance work, I would drop everything, no matter how inconvenient it was.

When the girls started school, I felt I needed to belong to an orchestra and, when I saw a second flute job going in the London Philharmonic, I knew I could do it. After an audition with eighty-one other applicants, I got the job.

I remember thinking that the LPO was a very serious orchestra, with very serious ideals, and I liked that – I was a serious player myself. That was ten years ago, and it is still a very serious orchestra.

In those days there weren't many women in the orchestra, maybe four or five. It's still a predominantly male set-up, and I have found it quite difficult to work with certain members of the woodwind section. It's taken me years to be accepted as the principal flute, not as 'that woman'.

For example, there could be a problem about how long to play notes in a certain phrase. I'd turn around to the bassoon or clarinet and say, 'What do you have printed at figure forty-nine?' And the principal clarinet would say, 'I'm not telling you – turn round.' This would be said jokingly, but it is still intimidating behaviour, and makes it quite difficult for me to persist.

When Jonathan, the other principal flute, talks to them, he doesn't get the same reply.

But all these sorts of things that happen to women are very strengthening. It's made me quite assertive. I'm determined to make sure I'm not treated as 'a jumped-up housewife' or something, because I'm not. I've worked bloody hard for that job.

There is an aspect of performance playing which is very solitary. As a principal, I have the first-flute part, nobody counts my bars for me. In a piece like Ravel's *Daphnis et Chloé*, for example, there is a massive flute solo, which can make or mar the performance. The two bars leading up to that solo are immensely lonely.

Like any instrument, the flute requires real extremes if you are going to perform well. Soloists require tremendous breathing capacity. I do breathing exercises when I've got a nasty solo coming up. Underwater swimming is very good, although I'm not a terribly watery person, so that's always an effort.

There are times when you're sitting on top of a high note, and it has to sound like a beautiful silver thread. You have to make a sustained dolce sound, and all the energy you require for athletic solos has to be got rid of. The French school of that era, Ravel, Debussy, produced beautiful, sensuous flute solos, and they are wonderful to play, because they lie in a region of the flute that brings out its really expressive qualities. When I play Ravel I get totally and utterly involved in what I am playing.

You get all sorts of wonderful moments in an orchestra. Being part of the collective sound can be tremendously exhilarating, you feel the energy coming from other players.

Often, there is magic produced by a conductor and the performing orchestra. I respond to conductors who have an intimate knowledge of the music, you have this feeling there is somebody on the podium who is really superior and who will draw out something really exciting, emotional, profound.

I did two performances of *Daphnis et Chloé* back in April for Zubin Mehta. When we first rehearsed it, we got to the flute solo, and he said, across the orchestra to me, 'I leave this entirely to you . . .' and I just thought, 'Thank you.'

The solo starts with a scale, and it's actually a moot point as to whether the scale has an E natural or an E sharp in it. We had two performances, and I played an E natural one night and an E sharp on the other, and we exchanged glances over that, right there in the performance. That sort of thing is very nice.

There are other conductors who give tremendous insights. Kurt Masur knows everything about Schumann, and he will draw out a very good performance. But he has very strong views and extremely exacting standards. For example, we recorded the 'Spring' Symphony, Schumann's First Symphony. It has a very florid flute solo in the first movement and it's hard, lots of cross fingerings, just the sort of thing you can trip over and make a mess of. The red light goes on, and there's me thinking, 'Help, hope this goes well.' We did a take, we did three takes, and they were all fine, but they were solid. '*Flaute*,' he says – other conductors might call you by your name – 'this solo, it must be *lustig, lustig*, very merry. Be brave, come on be brave.' And you think, 'Be brave? I was brave, I just did it three times.'

A conductor demands not just a good performance, but a really good one. He pushes you to your limit, he makes you explore, delve down into your box of tricks and try and find something else. Working for first-class conductors is very stretching.

As you can tell, I eat, drink, sleep, dream music. I feel very happy when I'm playing the flute in the orchestra. I feel that's where I am me, completely me.

Simon Channing

Flute

'It is something which fills you up and goes right down
to as far as it happens to be in you'

WHEN I WAS ABOUT EIGHT, I was taken into an orchestra
rehearsal at prep school and asked what instrument I fancied.
My best friend was playing the fiddle and I very nearly plumped
for that, but I chose the flute because it looked so different from
anything else and I liked the idea of playing it across, if nothing
else.

I didn't do any practice for about two years, didn't really move
from the football pitch, and then when I was about ten, I suddenly
found I loved playing it and really wanted to get going on it.

I won a music scholarship to Eton on the flute and started
practising very hard. But then I was taught English literature by
someone who was the most wonderful teacher and he completely
sparked me on that. I just put the flute down and, for some
years, I didn't know if I wanted to play it at all.

I got an instrumental scholarship to Cambridge and the flute
sort of tagged along. I had a great first year at Cambridge, but
it ended in an emotional crisis when my first girlfriend and I
split up. That somehow provided the release for my musical
energies. I suddenly thought, I must start playing the flute again.
I can remember playing the Poulenc Flute Sonata over and
over – a pretty lonely long vac I had, actually.

★   ★   ★

For six years I freelanced for the RPO and LSO, but then I did my first trial date with the LPO: the excitement of it, the buzz in the concert hall, I had never known anything like it. And from that day on I thought, I really do want to join this orchestra, because there is something happening here. I knew all the pieces really well for that night and yet I was incredibly on edge, a sense of nervous excitement.

At 7.30 p.m. on the dot you have to do a performance, and if you can't do it, you will be found out very quickly. That is one of the excitements of it – and why you're close to the edge all the time.

Of course, the nerve thing is not something musicians like to talk about. But everyone is prone to it. It is something that can hit you. I know. I had terrible nerve problems when I was about eighteen. I got a thing called lip shake, where I would put the flute to my lip and it would start dancing around, rather like a golfer getting the yips.

At the time, I thought I would never overcome it, and it got so bad that, even rehearsing on my own, I would be worried it would start happening. But gradually you overcome it, getting through a few more minutes without it happening, and now I know I have overcome it.

All the great composers have written wonderful music for the flute: Beethoven, Mozart, Stravinsky. Haydn's *Creation*, which we performed a couple of weeks ago, has wonderful woodwind writing in it, absolutely fantastic. There is a description of sunrise in it which has these chords gradually merging into each other and growing, and the flute sits on top of those chords, and they are absolutely sublime.

The conductor is fundamental. When you have a maestro standing on the box, he will get the orchestra playing to the peak of its form.

When Klaus is in front of the orchestra, something really quite incredible happens. I adore Tennstedt. Klaus seems permanently close to death, there is a feeling that this man has suffered. He is a difficult man sometimes, he has tantrums. But I feel a most incredible warmth and respect and love for him. Real love. There is nothing quite so touching as when you are in a concert and Klaus looks up at you, even in the midst of the most frenetic stuff, and catches your eye, and smiles – that is quite special.

Musicians in general don't talk in high-flown language about spiritual things, but they are spiritual. Musicians are plying a trade in which they are working with masterpieces; they spend a lot of their time in the presence of something which is manifestly bigger than them, greater than them, and that is an uplifting thing.

I find the more I am in the music business, the more I want to listen to music. Of course, you have a complicated relationship with music. Sometimes you think, God, I don't want to go to work today but, basically, I find this love of music to be something which deepens.

I would say music underpins everything in my life. I love being a musician. If I am without music for even a few days, I crave it like I am hungry. When there is a lack of it, I realize how strong is this desire for music.

If you love music, it permeates you completely. It is something which fills you up and goes right down to as far as it happens to be in you.

John Cobb

Personnel Manager

'John, where are we tomorrow . . . ?'

I USED TO PLAY the trombone. I was in the orchestra at the
Opera House for eight years and then, unfortunately, I lost the
use of my *embouchure*, and I had to pack in playing.

It was a gradual process, the production of the note gradually
deteriorated, and if the lip doesn't work it affects the brain . . .
until, in the end, I was absolutely petrified to go through the
stage door. I tried everything I knew to correct it, I had psychi-
atric treatment and hypnosis, but it never came back. I don't
know why it happened, I'd love to know.

I must say, I had some great colleagues; when I saw a solo
piece coming up which I knew I wasn't going to make, I'd nudge
the guy next to me, and he'd do it for me, so I got out of trouble
that way.

But, after a while, in each performance I was sitting there
petrified. I remember one night we were doing the *Ring*. I was
really struggling to hold it in there with the rest of them, and I
finally realized: 'I can't go on like this.'

I desperately wanted to stay in the business in some form or
another, and on one of my last dates, my desk partner told me
he had heard that the LPO wanted a personnel manager. And so
I applied for the job – and got it.

★　　★　　★

It's my job to make sure all the players are there with the right instruments at the right time, and I go to every rehearsal, every performance, every session. I also have to replace anybody who's off sick, or who has taken time off – this morning, for instance, the second bassoon rang in sick, and I've had to replace him for the performance on Thursday, which is *Petrushka*.

We have quite a few extras, and what little skill I have is in knowing who to go for: we obviously have high standards, and I know the players I can invite to play with the orchestra.

I always see the conductor at the start of the performance. There are things he might need which I can supply, such as cufflinks, dicky bows, socks, all manner of things have been requested over the years. Some are very tense, some are relaxed, but over the years you learn how to handle them. I just try, in my small way, to make them feel at ease and comfortable. If the hall is full, I'll encourage them by saying, 'We've got a very nice house, maestro . . .'

And then I'm there at the interval to see the conductor off the stage, so he's got a friendly face to walk off with. I am not normally sitting out in the auditorium, but I can hear the concert over the tannoy and, if I've enjoyed it, I tell him so. Then I get the orchestra back for the second half and collect the conductor from the changing room, ready to see him on again.

Well, I'm at an age now where there's nowhere much to go. I'm sixty-five and they could get rid of me any time they wanted.

I'd like to stay. I still feel fit enough and mentally young enough to continue for a few more years, so I hope Lord Luck's on my side, and they will allow me to continue. It's no hassle or problem for me to come to work – I enjoy it, I enjoy dealing with the ladies and gentlemen of the orchestra, and I hope I have a reasonable rapport with them.

The downside of my job is that I'm on call twenty-four hours a day. People pick up the phone and ask, 'John, do I need the piccolo tomorrow?' or 'do I need to bring the cor anglais?' They'll ring any time. They may have been out for a drink with the boys, and it gets to midnight, and I'll get a call: 'John, I can't remember, where are we tomorrow?' Very seldom does an evening pass where I don't get two or three calls.

But I like it all really, I have to say. I like the variety of life. You get the opportunity to travel, which is absolutely tremendous – there aren't many places we haven't been to since I've been here. It has all been very enjoyable.

I often regret that I'm not still playing. When I hear the guys out there really giving it the go, I would love to be able to do it. I still have a trombone at home and I try it from time to time, but it's so bad, I have to put it away again.

Cathy Craig
First Violins

'I wasn't going to take the money and run off to Bermuda'

I'M FROM THE MIDWEST of America, I was born in a town called Rockford, Illinois.

I'm not from a musical background, in fact my family was particularly non-musical. Nobody sang, nobody played an instrument, we didn't have a piano, the only thing we had was a record player.

My first musical experience was singing in the choir. My mother and father were active in the Methodist church, so it was kind of their churchly duty to have their daughter in the choir.

At school you could play a musical instrument if you wanted, and I elected to play violin. I thought it was such a cool instrument, I liked how it packed up, I liked the case, the cute little place where you put your rosin, I liked the little bow . . . I guess these are pretty non-musical reasons why I was drawn to the violin.

But when they were giving out the instruments, by the time they came to me, they didn't have any more violins left. The teacher said, 'Well, Cathy, you can play the cello, there's some nice cellos left.' So I played the cello, and liked the sound, it was a neat instrument . . . but my heart was really with the violin.

Six months on, the teacher said to the class, 'Today's swap day, and this is the absolute last time you'll be able to swap

41

instruments.' And I raised my hand and said I still wanted to swap. There was one violin left, the scraggiest instrument you've ever seen. It had only one E string, and it didn't have a nice case, there was nothing nice about it. It was a violin, though.

When I took it home, my mother was quite upset, she'd got used to the cello. But when my parents saw how keen I was on it, they were very supportive and found the best teacher in town, and I had two lessons a week. And then, all of a sudden, I was rising up the ranks, and I got to be pretty good.

I finished my education in New York City, where I got my Masters degree. To support myself, I would play in restaurants – Palm Court music mainly, which is violin and piano. There was 'Embraceable You' by George Gershwin, 'I've Got Rhythm' and 'Stardust' by Hoagy Carmichael, 'With a Song in My Heart' by Richard Rodgers . . . all with really quite complicated arrangements. It wasn't just a melody and the piano playing the filler, you actually had some technical, showy things for violin. 'Tea for Two', for example, has the most elaborate arrangement by Haifitz, with lots of double starts and harmonics and pizzicato. It starts off with a cadenza, and the melody is on the G string. Then you get a little technical flourish while the piano's playing, you then go into a waltz and, finally, you go back to the melody again. It's lovely.

I had to play for four hours at a go and I'd get a free dinner thrown in – as a poor student that really came in handy. Many times I'd get free drinks, and at the end of a set I would be quite tipsy.

It was all very good for my playing – the music, not the drinking – and I probably had a bigger repertoire then than I do today, because now I just read notes, there's nothing from memory any more.

I began playing with the American Philharmonic but, unfortunately, that folded. There was nothing to keep me in New York then, so I went to Lisbon, and became a member of the Gulbenkian Chamber Orchestra. And then my personal life became involved with my professional life, because I married a British clarinettist I met there. We both left the orchestra because we didn't like the conductor, and came to England, where we broke up . . . it was another woman. The music business isn't a good business to marry into.

There were a very lonely couple of years when I was first here. I was separated, I had no contacts, all I could do was rely on my playing ability, and hope that was going to earn enough to keep the house.

Anyway, I began freelancing, although I was determined to find a permanent job with a good orchestra. I also wanted to get out of playing in chamber orchestras, I'd had enough of Mozart, Haydn and Beethoven. I really wanted to get stuck into Strauss and Mahler.

It took five years, lots of auditions, lots of trials, and then I was offered a place in the LPO, and started last October. I was just about to give up on England – if I hadn't got that job when I did, I would have gone back to America.

I remember my first concert with the LPO. We did Mahler 10, with this English conductor called Wigglesworth. The funny thing about Mahler 10 is that Mahler didn't write all of it. The only thing that's pure Mahler is the Adagio. It's not often played, because it is very difficult; every bar has a different time signature. We had some rehearsals which didn't go well, and a dress rehearsal which was shockingly bad and, at that point, I told friends not to come to the concert. I didn't want to be embarrassed on stage.

I shouldn't have worried. It really was the concert of the year. The conductor conducted extremely well that night, and the orchestra just took the ball and ran with it, and it was staggeringly good.

I now have a Tugnoni, which is an old Italian instrument, from 1710, and it sounds about as far away as you could imagine from that scraggy violin I was given in Rockford Junior High. But I went through a lot of heartache to get this violin.

I had another Tugnoni on loan, which someone in the

profession was selling for £55,000, a huge amount. I tried to raise the money but just couldn't find it. I racked my brain to see what I could sell, I went to loan sharks, I'd re-mortgage the house. But after I'd had the violin for two months, I still couldn't get the money, so I gave it back to the owner.

Then a friend rang me up. He had just been to Sotheby's, and seen a Tugnoni, which was about to go on auction. So I raced over to Sotheby's, and I found that the Sotheby's violin was a much better sounding, healthier instrument than the one I had been trying.

That drove me crazy, I *really* wanted this one. I tried my neighbourhood bank, I tried re-mortgaging my house again, and it was no, no, no no no. And then Kathy Loynes, in my section, said, 'Try my bank manager in Baker Street.' There was only a week to go to the auction, so it was my last hope. I made an appointment for three o'clock Friday, and I also made an appointment for the morning at a bank in Wigmore Street, and I thought, I hoped . . . maybe, between the two? I was thinking, somebody's got to give me a loan – my career can't go on if I don't have a decent violin.

The first bank manager wasn't mean or anything, he just said no. He was even quite apologetic. I took all my papers off his desk, put them back in my folder and went to Burger King to wait for the next appointment.

When the appointed time arrived, we sat down, I took out my Sotheby's catalogue and showed him the picture of the violin. 'Miss Craig,' he said, 'have you approached any other institutions for a loan?'

I'm not a businesswoman. And I thought: what am I supposed to do? Say that just a couple of hours ago I was kicked out of NatWest because the manager didn't want to give me a loan? Anyway, after agonizing for a while, I said, '. . . No.' 'What about Wigmore Street this morning?' he said. And I just died. I looked over at that picture of the Tugnoni in the Sotheby's catalogue and thought, 'Bye bye.'

Then he wiped the floor with me. 'I don't know if I can do

business with someone who has betrayed me,' and, 'I don't know if you haven't just blotted your copybook enough that we can't do business.' I said, 'I'm very sorry,' and I moved to collect my things, and he went, 'No, no, just a minute, we'll see what we can do.'

Well, I guess in the end he thought I wasn't going to take the money and run off to Bermuda, that I was a serious musician. And he said, 'Go to the auction, don't worry about how much you have to bid, we don't want you to lose this violin.'

I bought it for £29,000, and it sounds great. You should come and listen.

Dermot Crehan
Principal, Second Violins

'It's harder and harder to get your enthusiasm going'

I COME FROM a very musical family in the west of Ireland. I was about four or five when I had my first fiddle thrown at me, and I immediately began belting out jigs and reels.

My father was absolutely mad about music, particularly Irish folk music, and he would bring me to all the different *feishes* and *flachios*. He taught me most of the folk music I know, and he played the tin whistle sometimes – we had a great old time playing together.

I also had a trio with my brother and sister, we did cabaret work in Dury's Hotel in Dublin, playing folk music. We were fifteen, fourteen and thirteen. We looked very sweet on the three fiddles; I think we sounded quite good as well. We won an International Opportunity Knocks, which got us a recording contract, and we got a few tours of the States out of that.

I went to the School of Music in Dublin where I had a very fine violin teacher, a Czech refugee called Jaroslav Vanecek. When he left, there was no one with whom I could continue my study on that level. People can only go so far in their musical careers in Ireland, and then they have to come to London.

Besides, it was getting just a little bit crowded around the house. I am the eldest of ten kids, and I was quite happy to leave.

I think a second-violin player is much maligned. They usually don't have the technical strengths first violinists have, that's why

47

they're second violinists. But second fiddles need to be pretty hot players. We're the real motor of the orchestra: while the firsts are running around the place, having a great time playing the tunes, we keep the music going.

We tend to be more down to earth than first-violin players, we are the 'get on with it' types, rather than the 'how am I playing today?' type. Less prima donna – probably a more acceptable bunch.

I always like going on tour. Denis Curlett, our trumpet player, brings the bodhrán, which is an Irish drum, and myself and Joe Maher, another Irish fiddle player, we find a nice bar somewhere, play a few tunes, and have a bit of a party. It gives everybody in the band a chance to have a sing-song, and blow off a bit of steam.

I have been enjoying the life, but I'm now beginning to get a bit tired, and I'm not that old – I was thirty-eight yesterday. It's just the sheer amount of work we have to do; we all work very hard and long hours, and we don't get that much time off. Also, the repetition gets to you after a while, you're just doing the same thing day in, day out. You can imagine, we're working together seven days a week, the same people, on the same platform, it gets very monotonous. After a while, it gets harder and harder to get your enthusiasm going.

I've got family demands as well. I have two very talented daughters who play the violin and cello, and they take up a lot of time. I do their practice with them before I go to work in the morning, and the other kids look like they are going to be very musical, too.

If I had time to do other aspects of music rather than play in the orchestra all the time, that would be fantastic: do some chamber music, play my Irish music. A little break from the orchestra would do me a power of good.

I'll have to try and wind it down a little bit, although if you take time off you lose money, we're only paid for what we do. But it's either that, or start to hate the business, and I don't want that to happen, because I love it so much.

Denis Curlett

Trumpet

'It would be a relief if someone said you can't play ever
again'

I WAS BROUGHT UP in an area called Newtown Abbey, which
is half way between Belfast and Carrickfergus as you go along
the Antrim coast. Life is hard in the back streets, it was just
survival. Fortunately, I had a bit of a talent for music, and I
played in the Belfast Youth Orchestra.

The kids in the neighbourhood would boot me around because
I was carrying an instrument, but it didn't bother me: 'I can do
something you can't, mate.'

I had to leave school at fifteen. There was no question of
staying on, as much as I wanted to. I worked on building sites
as a navvy for about five years. I used to take my cornet to work
and practise – anywhere I could find, in the building hut at
lunchtime, or sitting on the loo, or in the boiler house. The other
workers would take the mickey, they were ignoramuses.

At night, I went along to the Belfast Academy of Music, which
was a very upper-middle-class place. I would turn up in my
overalls and donkey jacket, as I hadn't got time to clean up and
change after work, and sit in a class with all these smart kids in
posh school uniforms, who would snigger and point at me.

But I had confidence, I knew I could play the trumpet. They
were just playing with it, it was just another amusement, a part
of their school activities. To me, it was my escape route out of
a pretty grubby existence which I hated.

When I was twenty-one, I was asked to enter a competition, which I won, and I was offered a scholarship to Trinity College.

After I left college, I joined the Hallé. The Hallé had a warm, lush sound at that time. They weren't the most accurate orchestra, but they could play things like Elgar and Brahms beautifully. I stayed there very happily for some years, and then I was asked to try out for the LPO, and came down to London for some trials.

The first thing I played with them was Shostakovich 10, with Haitink. Oh, it was sizzling – what a buzz! With a provincial band you get this wishy-washy, slightly lethargic performance, but these people really went at it, and the standard of playing was much higher. No matter what they may say about the Hallé, or any of the provincial orchestras, including Birmingham, they just don't have the quality of string playing of the LPO. Our first violin section is probably the best fiddle-player section in London.

I agonized over moving to London. My wife didn't want to come, but I said to her, 'If I don't take this job, I will die wondering' because everyone regards London as the pinnacle. They say if you get to London, you have made it.

But I have learned that is pie in the sky. At the end of the day, you are just sitting there scraping a piece of wood, or blowing down some tubing, and it wasn't long before I realized the quality of life in the provinces had been much better.

At least in the provinces you got one day off a week, but I have worked three month stretches here without having a single day off, and it has just worn me down. You end up feeling like you're on a production line. The Continental and American musicians have got time to themselves, and are looked after, they have job security, pensions, health schemes.

We don't get enough rest, or enough time to practise. If I am feeling really duff, I still crawl out to work, because if I don't go, I don't get paid. We have no sickness scheme now because the orchestra is in serious financial trouble, there's no holiday pay, there is no security whatsoever. I either work or we don't eat! When that sort of threat hangs over you, you don't feel secure. You certainly don't feel looked after.

Maybe I am at a mid-life crisis point, but I've lost sight of the music, it has literally got to that stage. I don't enjoy it any more. It would be a relief if somebody said, you can't play ever again.

Very rarely do we get great conductors, we can't afford them. Instead, we are working with mediocre conductors a lot of the time, and that drags you down.

This week we worked with the son of a famous conductor. He was nit-picking at pieces, it was like picking a sore – pick, pick, pick – until it bleeds. This chap just killed it stone dead, everything we did was boring and lifeless.

I remember doing Mahler 5 with Klaus Tennstedt, he used about a third of the rehearsal time, and the thing was electric. We worked with Cervalisch, a few months ago. He is a gentle-man. People like this have got intellect, they have served an apprenticeship, they have learned their craft over many years, and they get a mood, create a sound from the orchestra that is different from the rest of them.

Kid conductors seem to have come into the business. They win a competition and, suddenly, they get dates with orchestras like the LPO or the LSO, and they put that on their CV, and it looks very impressive. But they have got nothing to say about music. Any decent musician can learn to beat time and read through a piece, but for somebody to breathe a tangible bit of life into it – that is something these people can't do . . .

Franz came as a relative unknown to step in at the last minute, deputizing for Tennstedt. He had only conducted an Austrian youth orchestra before, and a very obscure little band in Sweden. He has a monotone voice, and he doesn't communicate terribly well. Also, he has got this thing about fast tempi. He takes things so damn fast that people can't play them, and he will not slow up. We did *Petrushka* last week, and it wasn't very good at all.

I am afraid we are not going anywhere with him, his performances are just not top-class performances. He doesn't get half the results of a Tennstedt or Zubin Mehta or Wolfgang Cervalisch or Kurt Masur, that ilk of conductor makes Franz look like an apprentice. We really need a more established conductor in charge to get our prestige back. I cannot see it happening with Franz.

Quite a few of the London bands are turning into glorified youth orchestras, with very self-centred youngsters not respecting the age and experience of the older players. A lot of the young players who come in now think all the old guys are useless, they say it quite openly. But to be a good musician, it is not enough to be a brilliant technician whizzing round the instrument. Some of the older people have been playing their repertoire for donkey's years with very big-name conductors, and they have a lot to offer. I feel sad that respect has gone out of the business.

I probably won't be here in five years, I don't want to be. I am just not happy doing what I am doing. I want to get away from London and back into the provinces.

I suppose I would miss the top-class conductors, you don't get that in the sticks. But even in London you see fewer of these people anyway, because no one can afford to pay them any more.

There are great financial worries for all the musicians in the LPO – I'm not the only one, we're all ridiculously overdrawn at the bank, getting hassled by bank managers. The management are clawing back 10 per cent of our salary at the moment, so we are just earning pennies – and you think, Christ, this is a so-called world-class orchestra!

The fact is that I am forty-six, and I should be comfortable by now, I should not be struggling to pay the bills. Instead, for the last five years, I have cut down on every expense I can think of. I eat sandwiches all the time, I brew my own beer. But with a wife who doesn't work, and a young family, I can't make ends meet, we are having trouble just trying to survive.

I never dreamt I'd be wealthy in this business, but I never thought I'd be as hard up as I am now.

★　　　★　　　★

I have never seen an orchestra with morale so low as ours is at the moment, it really is rock bottom. We still do good concerts, we are professionals, we will not drop our standards – if you put an orang-utan up there, we would still keep up a consistent standard. But we seem to have been badly let down by our management. No one has apologized for this mess we are now in, no one has said sorry. We are just expected to go out and play at a high standard the whole time . . .

Miranda Davis
Viola

'At least we get applause for coming to work'

I'VE GOT TWO OLDER sisters, one's a violinist and the other's a flute player, and my twin brother plays the cello. Music was a big part of my life from an early age, I didn't really think about doing anything else. I always practised a lot, and worked hard. I used to come home from school and do two hours' practice before doing my homework.

My father's a viola player too, in fact he often plays with the LPO as an extra. Dad is much more naturally talented than us lot, he's practically self-taught.

It was difficult when I became first extra. He was used to being first extra. The orchestra would ring up and say, 'Can we speak to Miranda?' Our diaries were next to each other on the table, and mine was full, and his was empty, and I felt really bad about that. We didn't talk about it, he's not very communicative in that way, but we worked through the problem.

When I first joined the LPO, there were no more than ten women, and I had to learn how to cope with being a young girl in an orchestra full of men.

It was quite difficult at first. The men were very curious about me, and when we went on tour, so many people wanted to talk to me I was exhausted most of the time. On the flights or coach rides I'd think, now I can just shut my eyes for a bit . . . but then someone would sit down next to me, and he would be asking me questions and, of course, you had to be friendly.

The life of an orchestral musician is a relentless schedule, you have to learn an enormous amount of music in a short space of time. You get to the concert, and because of the schedule you haven't had time to learn the music, and you just think, right, I've got to make the best of a bad job. And when you're absolutely exhausted, which I often am, there is no way you can get anything out of the music – your playing deteriorates.

Bruckner, who we're playing at the moment, is particularly hard, because he writes pages and pages of scrubbing, we call it, tremelendo, which is when you're at the end of the bow and moving it as fast as you can. That is very tiring and, also, because violas don't have the tune, it can be a bit boring.

I have a love/hate relationship with my viola. If I'm playing well, I can feel it's like a friend, but other times I can absolutely hate it.

Quite often, when the trombones are playing fortissimo, you can't even hear what you're playing – the audience certainly can't hear what you're doing – as long as your bow is moving no one would know if you're playing or not. In some orchestras, strings won't bother to learn those parts covered by the brass.

Earlier on, playing in an orchestra was a challenge, but it doesn't stimulate me now, I mean, once you have learnt a piece it becomes routine, you just go in and read the notes, you're like a sophisticated machine. Then I'll think, do I really want to carry on playing for the rest of my life?

I don't find it fulfilling or enriching any more. I would like to do more chamber music, or take an Arts degree – maybe change professions altogether. I pray the orchestra is not going to be for the rest of my life.

But, sometimes, I feel very privileged to be a musician. When we've done a very good concert, and the audience has cheered and clapped us, you think, at least we get applause for coming to work. That's very nice. Also, I would never have been to

Japan or many other countries if I wasn't in the orchestra.

When you're working with very special soloists or conductors, you feel privileged. A very good conductor makes all the difference. It's a bit like school: there are certain teachers who just have it, they walk into the classroom, and they command instant respect – and a conductor is a bit like that.

Mariss Jansons is my favourite. He has so much charisma, and he has lots of energy, which is great – some of the older conductors, musically they might be fantastic, but they are lacking in vitality. He's also got an incredibly good rehearsal technique. Most conductors just play the music through again and again in the hope that it is going to get better. Mariss Jansons hears when things aren't going right, he takes it apart, and he manages to isolate the difficult points.

One side of me thinks I could easily just give up music, and would like to, but it's a bit naïve to think it means that little to me. It is a big part of my life, without it I might be quite lost, I don't know . . .

Geoffrey Downs
Double Bass

'I couldn't even tell my wife I was a Barnardo's boy'

I DON'T KNOW how much you want to hear of my life, but my father died, leaving my mother with six children. My father was a metalworker, and when he got something in his eye at work, it turned to peritonitis, and his whole body became poisoned. I suppose with modern drugs he would never have died.

I was about four when I was put into Barnardo's. They tried to keep all my brothers together, but because of the demands of different ages and schooling, we did get separated.

Being a Barnardo's boy has caused me so much pain, and it's taken me many years to overcome. Do you know, when I got married, I couldn't even tell my wife I was a Barnardo's boy? It took years before I could talk to her about it, it was as though I was ashamed.

Can you imagine, at four years old, suddenly being placed in a strange place, and no one reasoning it out with you? The shock must be enormous. There was no one to help you get through this, there was no loving, no individual care and attention or anything. And my mother never once came to see us, all the time we were in the homes.

I don't have any bad feelings against my mother, I just think she couldn't cope.

You know, of all the time I was in Barnardo's, I only have

one tender memory. My youngest brother, Hubert his name is – although we call him Bert, because who wants to be called Hubert nowadays? – had a period when he suffered terribly with earache, and he used to cry at night. And I remember getting into bed beside him to comfort him. That's the only memory I have of closeness or emotional giving, and never receiving any.

When I was twelve, my grandmother arranged for us to meet our mother; I didn't have any feelings for her, it was just like going to meet Mrs Brown from up the street.

In later life, I did go and visit her a couple of times, but we didn't have any significant conversations, which I regret, because I would have loved to have heard her side of the story.

A few years ago I went into therapy, I had so much anger locked inside me about what had happened. And it's only within the last five or six years that I've actually become what I call a well-rounded person.

Let me say one last thing about Barnardo's; if you could meet my brothers, you would be impressed, they're all really nice, good people, and characters, all of them. And none of us has gone under.

I love music, always have done. When I was deciding what to do in my life, I thought, you only do people good playing music, you don't do any harm. It's a nice way to spend your life.

I've done the whole lot. I played in all the West End theatres, all the night clubs, I worked in the Astor Club, the Colony Club, I was at the Hammersmith Palais for two years, and at the Dorchester Hotel, playing in the restaurant. When I saw the London Philharmonic were advertising for bass players, I went along and did an audition, and very soon started to play with them.

When you play these lovely sonorous bass notes in a beautiful string passage, it's a wonderful feeling. It's so deep our instrument, people often don't realize. As a matter of fact, a low B string on a double bass vibrates so slowly, you can actually count the vibrations with the naked eye.

Old English basses are really fine, and I have one by a man called Fent. That's my pension. I will sell it when I pack up playing: I'll have to, because we'll need the money.

But I wouldn't let it go unless I liked the person. A man recently was pressing £20,000 into my hand. I didn't say I wouldn't sell it to him because I didn't like him, but that was the reality. I've got to like someone first . . . it's a very precious thing to have a bass like that, it's a very beautiful instrument.

Anyway, I don't have any immediate plans to pack it in. I'm sixty now, but I'm very fit, and I've still got a great enthusiasm and appetite for life.

I regard myself as an extremely fortunate person to have been able to play in an orchestra, and make a living the way I have done. It's given me so much, I have been to the most wonderful places, had the most wonderful experiences, and made friends all over the world.

You know, coming from nowhere, and having started with nothing, I've been very fortunate.

Robert Duncan
Viola

'Just because I have an interest in steam locomotives . . .'

APPARENTLY I COULD HUM tunes before I could speak – the
Beethoven violin concerto was a particular favourite. My parents
decided I might have some kind of ear for music and, one
day, my father brought a violin home, and lessons started from
there.

I also started playing the viola, and I played both instruments
until I was seventeen. Being large, I coped with it better than
the violin, and I liked the mellow middle-range sound of it better,
so I decided to stick to the viola.

I immersed myself in the viola repertoire. There aren't a lot of
solo pieces for viola and I found it very interesting to track down
the composers who particularly write for it. I like twentieth-
century composers like Hindemith, who was a viola player, his
harmonic language appeals to me. Unfortunately Hindemith is
not box office in this country, so he isn't played a lot.

Beethoven's late string quartets I find exciting to listen to, they
are very different from his symphonies, he has gone to another
dimension of expression in harmonic language. They were written when he was deaf, and you think, gosh, this is like Shostakovich, there is a sort of despairing quality in the music, which
may have been due to his condition.

★   ★   ★

I am also really interested in steam locomotives. I have travelled to places like Turkey, Poland and Hungary photographing them. It is incredibly exciting to see and hear them actually working.

Quite a few composers have been interested in them. Dvořák had a passionate interest in steam locomotives, he actually used to send out his students to find which particular locomotive was working a train from Prague. When Dvořák came to England, he liked to ride in the cabs of locomotives – in fact, he rode on The Mallard from King's Cross to Hitchin, which in 1936 was the fastest steam locomotive in the world at 126 mph, which it achieved during a test run on a short stretch south of Grantham.

Another composer, Arthur Honegger, wrote a piece called 'Pacific 231', which depicts the sound of a locomotive starting, and gradually getting faster and faster.

All the locos sound different, depending on the amount of cylinders they have. If it has got three, it will beat in three bar, if it has got four it will be in four – there is a real rhythm to it.

Recently, I travelled around various parts of East Germany photographing locomotives, some of them dating from before the Second World War. It is quite fascinating to see these things still running in ordinary service. There was one locomotive in East Germany that sounded particularly exciting. It was moving an enormous freight train, going very slowly, but with a very fast beat, and the sound of steam working hard up a gradient has this real feeling of power. It was part of Class 44, which they started building in 1926.

Just because I have an interest in steam locomotives, everyone expects me to know where particular trains go. People in the orchestra are always asking me, 'When is the train from so and so?' That does annoy me. There is someone in the cello section who does gen himself up on timetables, Roger Lunn, they should ask him.

Lawrie Evans

Principal Trumpet

'I was causing the neighbours very great concern . . .'

I WAS WELSH BORN, a long time ago, as you'll gather. Ours was a musical family. My dad was a singer in the Penderis – the Penderis Male Voice Choir – and he could also play the cornet and trombone.

There used to be a brass band in my little village of Ynyshir, near Pontypridd. All the kids from the valley were in this brass band, sixty of them – and only twenty-five instruments. So they gave the eldest members the instruments, and we youngsters were just given a mouthpiece, and had to learn all the fingerings for the scales. Only when you had learnt these skills were you then put on the instrument list.

I wanted to play the cornet so badly, and I practised the whole time. When I had done all the scales, the brass band gave me . . . a tenor horn. I remember bringing it home, absolutely in tears. But my parents saved up and bought me a cornet in Cardiff market. It was £8 that cornet: my dad was only earning £2 10s a week, he was a miner you see, so that was about three or four weeks' salary for him – he probably bought it on the hire purchase. Oh, it was like gold-plated diamonds to me. I gave back the tenor horn and cherished this cornet, which was mine, I loved it, and practised like mad.

In fact, I practised so much, our local policeman eventually came around and said I was causing the neighbours very great concern, because we lived in one of those big long terraces of houses, and of course the walls were very thin. In the end, my dad got an allotment half way up the mountainside, and it had a little chicken coop in it where I did my practice.

I got pretty good, and became principal cornet in our brass band, the Ynyshir & Motstar Youth Brass Band.

At eleven, I went to the grammar school in Ferndale. The headmaster there was very musical, and the maths teacher, Emlyn Thomas his name was, started an orchestra in the school.

I wasn't crazy about orchestras at that time, I was full of brass bands. However, I was infatuated with the headmaster's daughter, who played the viola, so I went along with it, and did my brass-band practice three times a week, and tried to fit in my schoolwork at other times.

I wanted to be a motor mechanic, I would have loved that, I was very interested in fast cars. I bought a Morgan, for £100, believe it or not. It did four miles to the gallon, and if you changed out of second gear, all the plugs oiled up.

My father wanted me to go into music, he wanted me to play the trumpet professionally. He said there was something special in me. I didn't think I could do it, I really didn't. So he said, 'Do the scholarship, if you don't get it, we will put you into engineering.' So we came to that agreement, and I did win the scholarship, and went to the Royal College of Music.

I joined the LPO twenty years ago. I really love playing the big, huge works, Bruckner and Wagner. I think all Mahler is so lovely – particularly conducted by Klaus Tennstedt. If you had to ask for my favourite complete work, I would say Mahler 9, if you asked me which bit of Mahler I love most, it would be a piece I'm not in, the slow movement of Mahler 5. Oh, I love that. The string sound is so fantastic, it tears my heart apart, it's absolutely marvellous.

★　　　★　　　★

I left home at 7 o'clock this morning for a 10.30 rehearsal, and I will be home after midnight, when everybody is in bed. It was my little girl's birthday, she's five today. I couldn't go to her birthday party, again. So what you can say is that I see far more of my colleagues than I do of my family. My first marriage broke up because of it. My wife went out with another man because she said she felt so lonely. That really upset me, it took me a long time to get over that.

My ex-wife has got my old cornet, and she won't give it back. I had four children by my first marriage, and I was trying to train my youngest son to play it just before I left home. But she said recently, 'that is the only thing he has got to remember you by,' and made me feel bad because I have always wanted it back. He never touches it, mind you, but she still won't give it back to me.

Now I have another two children by my second marriage; we are quite happy at times, but she also gets fed up because I am never there. I would like to be at home with my family, but I love the job, and if I didn't do it, I wouldn't be happy.

After a concert, particularly on tour, we have a great time. We do tend to over-drink, especially the brass section – I don't know why it always ends up in the brass section. On a free day we like to unwind. I mean, we are away from our families, we have nothing to do, and myself and a few other boys, we are not sightseers. Besides, we have done it all – I have been to Japan nine times, there is nothing I want to see there. We go up to our rooms and have a good time, or find a bar somewhere and have a laugh with the locals. Dermot plays the Irish music, and he will tell us which bar he's going to play, and we all pile in. That to me is far better than going round the temples, which you have seen before on the last trip, in any case.

Rachel Gledhill

Percussion

'You can shake it, you can bang it, you can hit it with
your fist or with your knee'

I'VE ALWAYS BEEN interested in hitting things. As a kid I used
to get the pots and pans out of the kitchen, and lay them out on
the floor and make a drum set of them. I kept asking Dad to
buy me a drum kit, but he was reluctant, because he thought I
might give it up after spending all that money. But in the end I
managed to persuade him – I think he fancied a go on it.

It's a very bandy area where I come from – it has two brass
bands – and Holmfirth High School, where I went, is a very
musical school with a really good standard. We did lots of exciting things, and we played at the National Festival of Music for
Youth, and that was really thrilling for us, coming from a little
Yorkshire town, and going down to London.

Eventually, I moved on to playing the tuned percussion, xylophone, glockenspiel and timps. That was a bit daunting, because
it's very different from playing the drums, you have to be a lot
more accurate where you hit it, because if you're just a centimetre
out, you hit the wrong note.

I've been in the LPO over a year now and I'm enjoying it a lot.
There are so many instruments which you are required to play
on an everyday basis in the orchestra. There is bass drum, cymbals, snare drum, triangle, tambourine, xylophone, glockenspiel,

tubular bells, marimba, vibraphone, tenor drum . . . lots. Fortunately, I like a variety, and I enjoy playing all of them.

You have got to be able to stand up on the platform and be on view, because whatever you play, it's always a solo part, and it stands out. Take the hammer blow in Mahler 6. You have to pick up this massive hammer in the middle of an almighty climax of music, and strike it right on the fortissimo chord. You have to have a bit of a go-for-it attitude, I think, and get used to making a fool of yourself.

There are often long passages of very loud playing, and then you have suddenly got to play quietly, and your heart is pumping, and the adrenaline is flowing, and sometimes your hands can start shaking, so you have got to be able to control that – you can't allow yourself to get too excited.

I get the impression that some people in the orchestra think percussionists are a bit of a joke. When you come off the stage, they will say, 'Oh, you had a hard night tonight with your triangle piece, didn't you?' while they have been strumming away all night on their violins.

But you can make a bad sound on a triangle, and when you hear somebody who makes a good sound, you think, 'God, I never knew it could sound like that!'

Many of the instruments we percussionists play are very difficult to master. The tambourine, for instance, well, that is quite a technical thing to play, because there are so many different ways of playing it. You can shake it, you can bang it, you can hit it with your fist or with your knee, or scrape your thumb round to make a roll. There are lots of different sounds as well, because you can vary the tension of the skin, and depending on whether you play on the wood at the edge, or the middle, or how many fingers you use, or what part of your hand, you can change the sound dramatically.

The cymbals are a lot harder to play than they look. You have got these two gigantic bits of metal wobbling around all over the place, and you have to try and get them exactly together and produce a neat, clean sound. And if you are not careful, you can produce an airlock – all the air gets sucked out between the cymbals, and it just goes, shlooooooop. Can you imagine? You are supposed to be playing a massive crash, in front of thousands of people, and you end up with a schloooooop . . . Aargh!

In Bruckner 7, there is one cymbal crash in the whole piece, and that cymbal crash is probably the most moving bit of it, so the way you play that crash can make or break the piece. So you have really got to know the music, and feel it, and you can be very moving in that context, just to use one example.

People don't seem to realize . . . but I am being rather defensive about it, aren't I? When you come and hear us, you'll see what I'm going on about.

David Godsell
Viola

'I don't really know to this day why they picked me'

EVER SINCE I can remember, I have wanted to be a musician, which was a funny thing really, because I didn't have the faintest idea what was involved. My father was a heavy manual labourer, he spent his time in a grain mill transferring sacks of barley from one place to another, and my mother had her own little milliner's shop.

I had fixed on learning the violin, and I joined the local rural music school in Trowbridge, Wiltshire. The instructor was rather a gorgon, she wore cable stockings of all things, and she hadn't the faintest idea how to teach. Every term when someone new came into the class, we went right back to basics, open strings, pizzicato, and so in three years I didn't learn a thing.

Another teacher came along and, recognizing I had some talent, recommended I had private lessons. I realized then how little I knew compared to other people. Funnily enough, at first my new teacher didn't realize how little I knew, because I was playing sharps and flats instinctively, without realizing there were such things as keys.

During the next year, she started teaching me theory, and I had a lovely time. I was a big lad, I was a whole six foot by the age of twelve, and she put me on to playing the viola, which was a much better thing really, it suited my size more.

Eventually, I managed to get lessons with professionals in

73

London. I'd come up on Sunday mornings from Trowbridge on the slow train, starting at 7.15 in the morning, and getting into Paddington at half past ten; it went through all sorts of stations that don't exist any more, Halt Junction, Twyford, Theale, through Devizes and places like that, it just stopped everywhere. But you will be talking to my desk partner, Roger Lunn, no doubt, who is a real puffer-train buff.

I went to the Royal College for one year, and then National Service interrupted things, and I went into the Grenadiers string orchestra. We were a strange sort of animal to the military mind, they didn't really know how to deal with us, because we were not subject to the discipline other guardsmen were. The people at our HQ in Wellington barracks were a bit resentful that we didn't fit into the military regime, so they were always trying to catch us out, and frequently gave us unexpected drills and inspections.

Whatever was required of us in the way of engagements, guard changings or investitures, we would go along and play, and after guild dinners we got a little extra money in with our wages.

We played selections like *King and I*, all the shows from the year dot, and we learned all the light music ways and mannerisms, and how to play a waltz beat. While we were there, *My Fair Lady* came on the scene, and we played that everywhere. That dates me doesn't it?

When I left the army, I had a letter, out of the blue, from the LPO, saying, would I be interested in a job with them? And I thought, well, yes, please. So I went down to the office and had a chat, and they said, 'When can you start?' I don't know to this day why or how they picked me.

Anyway, I joined the LPO nearly thirty years ago.

Number five, where I sit, is a good place to be. You are close enough to the front to be included on almost all the work that is going, but far enough back not to be on the front line.

At my age, I wouldn't like the responsibility of playing further up. Of course, I am capable of it, but it is a strain, and I don't want the limelight, I am not that sort of person. You have to have a killer instinct to cope with that day in, day out. I have had a taste of it, because the principal left when I got here, and I had six months as acting principal. But when you are young you can cope with it much better, you think you are Jack the Lad anyway at that age.

In the orchestra, I don't tend to associate with the people I sit down with, I think it's nice to get away from your desk partner, not because he is in any way objectionable, but because you are in each other's pocket otherwise. So I tend to form relationships with fiddle players or bass players.

Also, at my age, one tends to associate with the old timers. I am a lot older than the vast majority of the orchestra now; they come in from college, and I suddenly realize that that girl or that chappie is young enough to be my son or daughter!

Joan Graham
Cor Anglais

'I like being peaceful'

MY FATHER PLAYED the organ at church, this was a little mining town called Swadlincote, in Derbyshire, near Burton-upon-Trent. He had his own organ in the downstairs room, and he was always singing and playing music. He was potty, quite potty, and I adored him.

My brother played the trombone and double bass, but he suddenly came home one day and announced he was fed up and didn't want to do it any more – and now he repairs and makes clocks, and is very peaceful doing it too.

When I went to school, my dad said to me, 'What you want to do is play the oboe, our Joan.' So I went to the music teacher and said, 'I want to play the oboe, sir.' (I hadn't a clue what it looked like even.) 'Sorry,' he said, 'we haven't got any oboes, so take this flute and see how you get on.' And after a week I took it back and said, 'I don't want this, I want an oboe . . .' which is the worst thing I ever did, because to play the flute would have been much easier – there are no reeds to think about.

I never asked my father why he was so keen on the oboe. He is dead now, so I'll never know. Perhaps he just liked the sound of it.

Anyway, eventually, I got my oboe. It was a school one, a really ropey, terrible thing, which had been bashed around and misused, and not maintained properly. And then, when I was

77

fourteen, my parents bought me one for £98, and I have still got it. It is a beautiful old thing, with lovely silver keys.

I became principal oboe for a period of about three years, but it is a very pressurized job playing principal oboe. I found it all a bit too much. To start with, the first oboe always gives the A – the note which tunes the entire orchestra. So you've got to be there before everybody else, and make sure you are ready and in tune, you can't creep in late, or anything like that.

I just found, for my personality, being up front all the time didn't fit in with me. It made me very tense and stressed, rushing around and being niggly. And I like to be peaceful. I said to myself, 'I can't go on like this', and I chose the cor anglais, which is a larger version of the oboe, and I just do that now.

I like it, it is more peaceful. It is a fifth lower in pitch, and has a big bell, which gives it a very deep, dark, rich sound. The cor anglais is used for all those dark, rather gloomy introspective solos like Shostakovich. I like playing Shostakovich on it, I like playing everything on it, actually, I find I can express myself through the cor anglais.

Also, I don't know how you can say it without sounding really soppy, but maybe when I play, I am expressing a love for Derbyshire, and my dad, and all that.

But you do have to be making reeds all the time. I can't stand them. You have to carefully scrape them with a knife until you get each one to vibrate the way you want it to, which takes hours, and you get through them quite a lot, particularly the amount we are playing, often six to nine hours a day.

When I have a big solo to play, for about a week beforehand it will be on my mind, and then it is a relief to get to the concert and get stuck in.

Next week we have got the Berlioz Fantastic Symphony, and the cor anglais just plays in the third movement. So I have to sit for two whole movements doing nothing; then there is this arty-farty thing where I am supposed to be 'the shepherd looking after his sheep'. There is an echo off stage, which is an oboe, and then it is just me playing, echoed again by the off-stage oboe; then there is a bit of very quiet shimmering strings going on, and just me, and a bit of timpani roll, and just me again. It is all very exposed for one movement. And then for the rest of the symphony, I just sit there and twiddle my thumbs. There is a lot of that when you play the cor anglais, sitting around waiting. But the brass are behind, the viola players are directly in front of me, and you hear the orchestra like you never hear it on CD or watching a concert; it is very exciting. I enjoy sitting there.

The conductor's personality and technique is very important. Someone like Klaus Tennstedt is amazing. He sways about on rickety old legs and gets the most amazing performances somehow. He is incredibly musical, and he always chooses the right tempo for everything, which a lot of conductors don't.

I shouldn't be living in London at all. The Derbyshire bit is the real me. I feel very strongly that my roots are up there, it is the place where I feel really free and happy, walking on my own. Does that sound stupid?

It is good to get away from the oboe, it really is. But it is never away from my thoughts, and when there is a big solo coming up, it is important to keep myself in trim, and make sure all my reeds are sorted out.

If I could just take it out of the case every morning like a flute, and know it is going to be the same as it was yesterday, that would be so brilliant. It is a great worry, this reed thing, you have to be prepared for any eventuality: if the humidity or the temperature changes, you might have to change a reed in the middle of a concert. I have got six reeds which I am nurturing along at the moment, and a couple that are currently in playing mode. And I shall have to make some more when you are gone.

Oh, it is an awful chore . . . that really is the worst part about playing the oboe.

Ken Graham

Stage Manager

'I've got a big Renault, with double-twin bunks . . .'

I'M THE STAGE MANAGER. Basically, I'm concerned with getting the instruments from venue to venue, and setting the stage. All the large instruments, the double basses, percussion, brass, plus all the furniture that needs moving, like stools and chairs, go into my trailer, which is thirty-five feet long.

The timpani are the trickiest instruments to deal with, they're awkward to lift, because of the odd shapes, and they're heavy. There's one wretched timp which is 120 kilos – most people couldn't even lift some of the things I have to carry. You have to be fit, there's no two ways about it.

I've got a big Renault, with double-twin bunks, and a full CD system. You could live in it, it's a home away from home. It's temperature controlled too, you can't have just any old thing, there's a million pounds worth of instruments in that trailer when it's loaded.

We often have a three-tier day, which means we start in the Festival Hall for rehearsal, go to an afternoon recording session, say at Abbey Road, and then a concert back at the Festival Hall. That's quite a few trips backwards and forwards from the truck, and you don't get very long to do the moves either.

Having worked for the LPO for a long time, I'd known Joan for years, but we were on tour, and one night in Munich something clicked, and we never looked back – and got married shortly after.

It's great now because when we go on tour, we're with each other all the time, it's undoubtedly better that way. Looking back, I can understand the frustrations of my first wife, the long, unsocial hours, working weekends and evenings, it doesn't bode well for a good marriage.

I married at a very early age too, I had three children by the time I was twenty. Some people might say it was irresponsible, but they've all turned out okay.

When I see the orchestra on stage playing, I sometimes wish I could be up there too. I've always wanted to play the piano – just to sit down and tinkle out a tune would be great – but I never got around to it, and I fell out with the music teacher when I was at school, unfortunately. But I've seen the nerves Joan has to go through before a solo piece, and I don't think I'd like to put up with that.

The most nerve wracking thing I have to do is get on stage in front of the public if I have to set the stage between pro-grammes. Then I have to get out of my dirty jeans, change into a dinner jacket and bow tie and go out and rearrange the stage. Sometimes the audience will clap me, it's all very good-natured.

Because there is a lot of hanging around during the concert, I'll often sneak in and listen. One of the best concerts was Mahler 8, with Tennstedt, it was very emotional, and Klaus came off the stage totally drained. That was a really good night, it sent a tingle down my spine, especially knowing that I was responsible for getting all the instruments there. There's quite a bit of job satisfaction in this line of work.

Judith Grahame
Marketing Director

'He was married, living with his wife and kids . . .'

WELL, I HAD an unhappy marriage, with two children in their early teens. I had decided I was going to separate from my husband, but I would wait until both children had left home. So, in the interim, my game plan was that I would fill up my life doing work I felt was interesting.

I saw a job advertised at the London Philharmonic: it was their fiftieth anniversary and they needed someone to stuff envelopes and help with the publicity. It was the lowest of the low.

There was a disastrous interview, because they asked me to type something, and I couldn't turn the typewriter on but, anyhow, I got the job and, in fact, I was paid less than my daily woman.

I had never worked full-time before, I'd never been on the tube, and it was quite a culture shock. The first week I staggered home and went to bed about seven o'clock each night.

It was like working in a huge fog, every now and again it would shift, and you would get a tiny glimpse of what the horizon was, but otherwise it was a complete mystery to me what was going on. I knew the orchestra was desperately short of money, and they were putting on concerts which people didn't come to, which cost them an absolute fortune.

At Christmas, the managing director, who up until that time had never said a word to me, took me out for lunch, and announced that my boss was pregnant, and he wanted me to replace her.

I didn't understand the orchestra. The orchestra is self-governing, which means that the players are the shareholders, and they own the orchestra. They employed a management to ,run it and, when times were bad, as they were then, they'd say the management was ineffective – perhaps it was, I don't know. There seemed to be very little communication between the office and the orchestra, and what communication there was seemed to be full of fear and suspicion.

The chairman and the managing director didn't get on at all, they just had completely different ideas about how the company should be run. And if I've learned anything with the LPO, it is absolutely vital that the chairman and managing director have a good working relationship, because the chairman is the link between the administration and the orchestra.

I have got a practical nature, and I decided I could do my job best by concentrating on Klaus Tennstedt, who was just taking over from Solti as the principal conductor. There had never been a happy relationship between Solti and the LPO, whereas with Tennstedt it has always been described as a love affair. Knowing that, it seemed sensible to try and build on it, because the public is very interested in the relationship between the conductor and the orchestra. I spent quite a lot of time going to rehearsals and concerts, watching how Tennstedt was with the orchestra.

I went to Hong Kong and Japan with the orchestra, and I can remember sitting in a rehearsal hearing Klaus doing Mahler 5, thinking, I am being paid to come and hear this wonderful music, it's just a fantastic experience.

After a tour of Australia, I had some photos which I was looking at in the kitchen, and my husband came over. 'You look different,' he said. 'What's different about you in these photographs?' Then he suddenly looked at me and said, 'I know what's different, you're happy . . .' And I *had* been very happy on that tour, and had a wonderful time.

The orchestra showed that I could be good at something. I'd found a job I was obviously suited to. And that was very good for my self-confidence, it was something I'd done, rather than my husband, or my father, or anyone else. And when my husband left, it was an absolute relief that he was out of the way, from the moment he went it was as if he had never been in my life at all – although I was still very concerned and attached to my children.

I didn't get on with the new chairman, he made me cry in front of the orchestra. I went to see Tennstedt, and he sat me down, and made me give him my word that I wouldn't leave the orchestra until the new managing director was in place, who was going to be John Willans. I promised Klaus I would stay until he joined, and then see what happened.

Of course, when John came, it was a breath of fresh air. He was extremely supportive of what I was trying to do, and he gave me a huge amount of responsibility. I was made marketing manager, and I was asked to write a business plan for the orchestra. I went up to Cranfield Business School in a panic, but everything fell into place, and I just sort of flourished.

I suppose it was the normal, corny office relationship. I spent a lot of time working with John in the office, and I liked what was happening professionally, and I liked him. In September, we drove up to the Edinburgh Festival and spent some time together, and that's when I first became aware that he liked me. He was married, living with his wife and kids, but over the next nine months he started to talk to me an awful lot about what was happening at home. And then the following Easter he bought a narrowboat, and I went and stayed with him on the boat, and our relationship developed.

It was rather detached at the beginning: we are having an affair, but this is absolutely nothing to do with our professional lives. He remained married and I was going out with other people. This continued until I suddenly realized I was becoming very attached to him, and I then told him either it must stop, or I must leave the orchestra. He said I was too valuable at the orchestra, and we would just have to stop the relationship.

The following autumn, I met this man who lived in Paris and I told John I was going to stay with him. John went absolutely berserk and, in the end, I didn't see the other man, and John moved in with me.

I wouldn't recommend that situation to anyone. John was absolutely obsessed that the orchestra shouldn't know about our affair, apart from which, initially, his wife didn't know. There were all these silly little things: coming into the office in the morning, John would drop me off on the corner, and I would have to walk around the block before going in. But John was absolutely neurotic about us, he refused to make it official. Also, he was always very hard on me at work because he was concerned he shouldn't be seen showing favouritism, and I found that difficult. I'm sure everyone must have known anyway what was going on.

And then I was headhunted by a company who offered me a great deal of money to go and work for them, and John just blackmailed me: he said he needed me at the orchestra, and that if I left he wouldn't see me any more. So I stayed. I was terribly unhappy with that blackmail, but I was much more concerned to have my relationship with John than anything else.

We didn't make it public until last October. There was a hell of a fuss then, and there was quite a lot written about our affair in the papers. Four player directors resigned from the playing board, which meant there was no orchestra board. We, therefore, had to call an extraordinary general meeting to re-elect a new board, and it became apparent that at that meeting someone was going to use our relationship in an unpleasant way.

John and I both decided we weren't prepared to let that happen, because as far as we were concerned, professionally, there had never been anything wrong in the way we behaved. So John sacked me, and I left very quickly, literally at the end of the month. But he put me on a contract to handle the press and PR of the orchestra, and everyone seemed quite happy with that.

It took me about six months to adjust, because I was quite upset about the way I'd gone, and I felt I had done quite a lot for the orchestra. But, in fact it was the best thing that could have happened. It was just such a relief not to have to pretend any more.

I absolutely love what I'm doing now. I have good press contacts, I like working with the press, and I can now go to concerts with John quite openly as his companion.

I think the London Philharmonic changed me completely, but I think I was waiting to be changed.

Tina Gruenberg
Sub-principal, First Violins

'Just get rid of the bastard . . .'

I WENT TO THE ACADEMY at sixteen, I won a scholarship there. I absolutely loved my Academy days, and I found it so exciting to be with other musicians. And then, in my third year, I met Charles and we got married. It was just lovely to meet somebody so nice – my knight in shining armour.

Suddenly, Charles was offered a wonderful job as principal baritone in the Vienna State Opera, and I just wanted to be with him. You could say I left the country for him. A lot of people told me I shouldn't: 'You are at the threshold of your career, don't give it up to go to Vienna,' but the thought of him going, and my not being with him, well, it was just unbearable.

And Charles wanted me to come. I don't think he could have survived without me there really.

We had a sweet little flat in the old French quarter, which is a lovely bit of Vienna. Charles used to be free most afternoons or evenings, and we would take the car and go off to all sorts of places.

One day, I got a phone call from the Trio Zingara, who are based in London, and they offered me a job, which meant I had to fly back and forth the whole time. It was very difficult to be separated from Charles. The farewell scenes at the airport were so tearful, they became a standing joke with all the customs officers, but it was heartbreaking to be without each other.

Vienna ended because Charles's job, although very good, wasn't going to lead him to major roles there, so he thought he would try and find work in London. That's when I joined the LPO.

I can't believe I waited ten years to play in a professional orchestra. I have never been happier musically. I am playing with great conductors the whole time, it is so exciting to play these big symphonies, Beethoven 7 with Tennstedt is inspirational. I adore Klaus: I want to cuddle him, he is just so vulnerable and frail.

I'm afraid I giggle quite a lot on stage when something silly happens. Bob St John Wright, who sits next to me, his string broke in Shostakovich 5 the other night. He was on the E string, and suddenly it snapped, and he wouldn't stop playing to put another one on, and it was a passage which was so high, that in order to play it on the A string, he was practically scratching his nose. That sort of thing makes me laugh. People clown around sometimes, if you have a pizzicato passage, and your bow in your lap – somebody might just swipe it away.

I have a very beautiful instrument, my Rogère, Jean Baptiste Rogère, I am very lucky to have it. It was made in 1696, and is absolutely beautiful. It is my friend, my great friend. After a concert, I tell it, 'You have done really well!' and I put it to bed every night, and wrap it up in its cover. It has got real power, an amazing quality. The conductors demand so much sound that you think you are going to break it, but I always know it will give me that little bit more. I would be lost without it, absolutely lost, it is the most beautiful instrument I have ever seen.

I must also tell you about my dog, little old Béla Bartok. I always wanted a dog. I wanted a dog so much that when I was a child, I used to have a little plastic poodle which I would take to Hampstead Heath, and make it stop to pee at trees. Mind you, I don't see Béla as a dog – he is a puli, and pulis really are far more intelligent than other dogs: most dogs take twelve or fifteen commands, and a puli takes seventy-five. He is like a bear, a woolly brown bear. I adored Béla.

When Charles and I separated, Béla went, but I want him back now, I want them both back.

I made some mistakes. I fell in love with a man who pretended to be really nice, and then I suffered a lot, a hell of a lot. I don't think I deserve what has happened to me.

I didn't realize until it was too late . . . Charles really was almost perfect, I thought all men did things like that for their wives, but they don't. He was terribly, terribly nice, and Angus★ isn't.

Charles was so quick and bright, I couldn't keep up with Charles, but he never patronized me, and he had a love of everything, whereas Angus hates so many things.

I am still seeing Angus, out of desperation, I think. I don't know how to get rid of him. I keep saying, 'It is finished, I don't want to see you any more . . .' But then I feel responsible, because he left his wife for me, although their marriage was bad. Very early on, I wanted to go back to Charles, but Angus seemed to need me more, and then by the time I had made up my mind, it was a bit too late, poor old Charles wasn't going to go on waiting any more.

I tried for a reconciliation, and Charles wouldn't change his mind. He had waited so long for me, and he was so devoted to me, I mean, there was nothing casual about our marriage.

I don't like Angus very much. I know it sounds pathetic, but just occasionally it is company, and sometimes I think he is better than nothing – although I really know that nothing is better than him. But then I'll suddenly think, 'My God, what if I am alone for the rest of my life?' and then I decide that I had better stay with him until I get somebody else. It's complete insecurity, I know. I panic a little at my age. I would tell anyone else, 'Just get rid of the bastard and be on your own, you should get on with the rest of your life . . .'

★This name had been changed.

Colin Harrison
First Violins

'You, you, you, and why not, you . . .'

I STARTED MUSIC totally by chance. One day in the infant school, a teacher came into our classroom and said, 'I am the new viola teacher' – nobody knew what a viola was – 'and I need four people.' And he just turned round, and went, 'You, you, you, and why not, you.' (I was the third you.) They gave me a huge viola to play, I could hardly hold the thing, but after about a year, my younger sister brought a violin home from her school, and I tried that and found it much more comfortable.

From then on I started practising the violin, without telling the teacher, and one day I went to him with the second movement of the Tchaikovsky concerto, which I had prepared on my own. He was absolutely flabbergasted and suggested I go to music school.

For ten years I was studying and working in Germany – I was engaged to a girl there whose family came from Danzig – and I looked in the *Telegraph* one day and saw a violin position was vacant at the LPO, and decided to apply.

They wrote back and asked if I could come over and play for them, which I did. I chose Mozart's A Major Concerto, followed by Sibelius's Concerto, First Movement. It wasn't a great audition, perhaps because I had just flown in, and I wasn't really feeling up to it. I went back to Germany the same day.

But they offered me a trial, and I came across for two weeks, which was a very busy patch for the orchestra, and they offered me the job after that, and I was delighted to accept.

Officially, I am seventh violin, but I auditioned two weeks ago for number six. I played the same programme as four years ago when I joined. Well, why not? I have so little time to practise, and I thought it best to play safe.

I spent three solid weeks working on these pieces, it took that long to prepare. If you are playing orchestra repertoire the whole time, you get out of the routine of practising solo pieces. I still knew them from memory, but my fingers didn't know them any more, put it that way.

First of all, I went through everything very slowly, just listening for intonation and cleanliness, and once I felt a bit secure with that, I started speeding it up with a metronome. When I got up to tempo, I began thinking about the shape of the piece, and how I wanted to play it musically.

With the Mozart, I don't like playing it as a romantic piece; many people do, and I think that is quite wrong, because Mozart is not from the romantic period. I like Mozart to sound quite simple and classic, not too much vibrato.

As for the Sibelius Concerto, it is a terribly difficult piece technically. There are runs way up on the G string, there are nasty arpeggios, horrible chords to play, and it has all got to be clean, otherwise it sounds absolutely dreadful.

Anyway, it was the best audition I have ever done. Franz was there, and Joakim, and Bob Truman, the principal cello, who said I should be given the job straightaway. Franz was very complimentary, he said, 'I really enjoyed that, and I thought the Sibelius was stunning.' So I think I probably will get the job . . .

We are intending to have another child, but even though I really enjoy the LPO, it is not the greatest of jobs financially. I am thinking of going back to Germany for a better paid position – it is just a thought at the moment, but it is a possibility.

I suppose it always comes down to finance. The yearly salary is not that low here, it is just that for the amount of work we do, it is not well paid. I did well over 400 calls last year, and I earned about £32,000. You only get more money if you sit one, two, three or four in the section, otherwise, your salary stays the same forever. I sit four fairly often, but most of the time I am just on a *tutti* – rank-and-file – salary.

The other night I listened to the New York Philharmonic, who are at the end of a long European tour. They sounded very classy.

Orchestras like the New York Philharmonic and the Berlin Philharmonic have time to practise. They are paid a very good salary as well, and under those circumstances, you can keep up your playing pretty well.

I would like our orchestra not to be working seven days a week all the time, we need a few days off, time to practise, a pension. I only have time to practise concertos if I take time off work, which costs money.

Musically, there is room for improvement at the LPO. Lots of people have been in the band for many, many years, and they don't play as well as they used to. Overall standards in the music world have gone up markedly in the last few years, you can almost guarantee anybody joining now is going to play better than the chaps who have been there for the last thirty years. Also, better teachers are coming to England now, you never used to have these teachers, which is why I went to study abroad.

If the old timers were to audition today, they wouldn't have a hope.

Nevertheless, you can't start kicking people out, it is not the way we operate. Sometimes, violinists who started out in the firsts get pushed back to the second fiddles, which is easier for them, not so exposed.

But it doesn't make for a great orchestra if you have got a lot of dead wood. That is what holds us back from becoming one of the world's great orchestras, because there are some really classy players in the orchestra, some great players.

NOTE:

Colin passed the audition and is now playing at number six.

Peter Harvey

Trombone

'Always hiding behind the trombone . . .'

I ALWAYS LIKED the sound of the big bands. Don Lusher used to play sweet trombone solos, and I thought: oh, yes! *I* will play the trombone.

My teacher was a very old man in a waistcoat; he played the valve G trombone in a brass band, and there was something about him that completely mesmerized me. His life was so different from mine: he had music, and I could see the possibilities. He had to teach me what a crotchet was, I knew nothing at all. It took me two weeks to play a note, I obviously wasn't naturally gifted, but as soon as I had got a few notes, I was absolutely hooked.

The trombone was the only thing I could do. That is what drove me, I had nothing else. I was a fat boy, and I was lazy, physically I was not very attractive. I found schoolwork hard and boring, and I avoided games, but I loved the trombone, and I put all my energies into that.

I don't think I ever really matured as a person, because I was always so narrow-minded about the trombone.

I was disastrous with girls, I just didn't know how to handle them at all, and I was completely inarticulate.

At sixteen I was playing full time in a trad. band. I was playing at dances so I didn't have to dance: when I should have been dating girls, I was hiding from them, always hiding behind the trombone.

My first marriage was fairly disastrous. I had been looking for a wife; I suppose I was lonely. I wanted a mother figure, and I found one, and got married. She was very insecure herself, plus she was on the rebound. There was not a lot of love in our marriage. I almost left her on the honeymoon to come home, it was that bad.

The trombone was the one thing that saved me. It got me out of the house, it took me on tour, it kept me away and doing things. When we had children, I realized it wasn't going to work out. We had ten years, and then I left.

I met someone at Glyndebourne. I am hopeless at women, as I said. The only way I could chat her up was to get blind drunk, so I had bottles of rum in my pocket to keep things going. I just wanted a dalliance, something to prove I could actually attract a woman, but of course I fell in love straightaway, and we have been married for eight years.

Eliza is completely different from me. She has come from an almost county family, her father is a bank manager. She knows conductors, she knows a lot of wealthy, interesting people. She was all the things I wasn't, articulate, organized, slightly bossy. All I had was the trombone, but I realized the trombone wasn't going to get me anywhere with her. I had to learn to stand on my own two feet, to step in front of my trombone, which has been very difficult, but very good for me.

It was also at Glyndebourne I noticed this thing called nature.

There is a pub called the Trevor Arms, where the musicians always go in the interval at the opera. One evening I looked out in the garden, and there were some highly coloured birds, black and yellow bodies with the most vivid red spot on the top of their heads – I didn't realize then they were goldfinches. And as I looked at these birds on the lawn, I thought, wow, look at those colours! It was a real revelation. I suddenly realized how much I'd missed in my life . . . all that wasted time.

I am an avid birdwatcher now, I just love it. On tour with

the orchestra, anywhere in the world, when we have a day off, you don't see me for dust, I'm in a taxi a hundred miles up the road, looking for birds. At home I go out at 5 o'clock every morning. Through birdwatching I have learnt so much about plants and animals and life, I am just hooked on it. There's so much to see.

The reservoir near where we live is full of birds, which is part of the reason for living there. I walk up the lane with a telescope, and I can span it in about five minutes. In the marshes you see all these waders. When you look at them from a distance they look dull brown, and yet through the telescope you can see there are incredibly bright markings on them.

I am only forty-seven, but as you get older, playing becomes harder. It is a young man's business. I would love to get out and do something else. I could be a teacher one day, and a bird-watcher the next, or maybe become a volunteer warden, which I do a bit now. There is a nature reserve on top of the Downs where I count the birds in the early mornings during the spring, and I love doing that.

But I will probably stay in the orchestra, because I can't think of anything else to do, and no one is going to pay me to watch birds.

Fiona Higham
Second Violins

'There was wonderful eye contact between us'

MY FATHER WAS a frustrated musician all his life. He had a
very tyrannical Victorian father who wouldn't allow him to have
music lessons, but he taught himself piano, against his father's
wishes, and later, he encouraged me. He had a lot of musician
friends, and they were always coming round and playing our
piano, and so we had a very musical atmosphere at home.

My father committed suicide when I was sixteen, which was
a big shock, and rather a blow in the middle of O-levels. We
knew he was very depressed, he had been in and out of hospital
having electric-shock therapy, and everybody thought he was
getting better. But he went upstairs after lunch one afternoon
and attached a drip to his arm . . .

That had a big effect on my personal relationships. I didn't want
to trust any men after that for a very long time, and I had lots
and lots of flings. I wasn't looking for a serious relationship, I
probably wasn't capable of one.

Most of the men were musicians. There was an affair with
one conductor I had worked with, which went on longer than
most, but perhaps it was more to do with a father-figure thing,
because he was quite a lot older than me.

There came a definite point where I thought, there is something missing in my life, I actually want to have a long-term

relationship with somebody and, shortly after that, I met Jim, who was great.

That came to a crunch point after I got my job in the orchestra; because things had settled down in my life, I decided I wanted to have children. Then Jim wasn't ready to be committed. Most horn players don't like to be tied down, I think it is something to do with the fact that the horn is such an unpredictable, dangerous instrument to play.

Anyway, I said to him, 'You have got to make a decision one way or the other,' and he replied, 'I can't, so I had better go . . .' I was devastated, but at the same time I was determined I was not going to ask him to come back on any other terms.

About three or four months later, he started going out with a harpist, who he now lives with – and the irony is that she already had a child, so he has a ready-made family now, although he didn't want to make that big commitment to me.

A few months after Jim left, Constantin came on trial as leader of the orchestra. Everybody was completely bowled over by his playing.

I was sitting on the second desk of the second violins, and there was wonderful eye contact between us when we were playing. I can't explain it, and it wasn't put into words for quite a long time, but there was something between us, and, basically, from the moment we met, things weren't the same again.

I don't know exactly what it was that I found attractive, because he wasn't the type of man I would normally find attractive. He is very Slovak-looking, dark-skinned, and quite solidly built, not to say fat. But the way he played the violin, well, that was obviously a factor, I admired his playing a lot.

He was married, and I knew that, and I was quite determined I wasn't going to have an affair with him, because I wasn't interested in that kind of relationship any more.

But that summer, he said, 'Come and visit me.' So I went to visit him in Belgium, where he lived. I had no idea whether his wife would be there or not – she wasn't, actually, and he told me he felt very strongly about me. I said the same, but I told him I wasn't prepared to have an affair, so it was kind of stalemate, and we just left it like that. I came back to England, and I didn't hear from him until he came back to join the orchestra.

I had really thought nothing was going to happen, but the moment he arrived, that was it, we did start having an affair, but he was absolutely adamant that he couldn't leave his wife. She had come over to London with him, and they were in the process of buying a house, which he even took me to see before he bought it.

After a few months, Franz was appointed resident conductor, and that, I think, was the beginning of a real problem . . . Franz obviously needed to put his stamp on the orchestra, and he hadn't chosen the leader, Constantin.

Franz's first concert with us was in Linz, his home town. He was very nervous, and the concert didn't go terribly well. I particularly remember the 'Scottish' Symphony got very out of control and nearly fell apart. Franz liked to do things a lot faster in concerts than in rehearsal, which is fine most of the time, but sometimes a bit dangerous. Nothing dreadful happened, but it wasn't a very comfortable concert to do, and I think he put the blame on Constantin.

And shortly after that, Constantin was sacked, and given three months' notice.

I felt very hurt that people didn't really bother to stick up for Constantin, because they would have done it for other people. But I now understand that a lot of the orchestra were very resentful that they'd had no access to Constantin because he was always with me.

But because he was living with his wife, the only time *we* could be together was when we were at work, so every break, every lunch, and every dinner, we were together.

★   ★   ★

The main thing I have left out of this story is that when he was sacked, I was five months pregnant – which was planned, it wasn't an accident – Constantin and I wanted to have a child. The orchestra didn't know, because I had kept it a secret.

All this time, Constantin was still living with his wife, he felt he couldn't leave her. I suppose he hoped she would find out and leave him. But although she must have known what was going on, she refused to face it, she just buried her head in the sand. I said to Constantin, 'It is not fair on her,' and I actually made him tell her.

Anyway, that is all in the past. Constantin is now divorced, and he lives with me. He was trying for the last year to get another job, which had been very difficult because his reputation was seriously damaged by what happened in the LPO.

It has all worked out very well, because Constantin has just got a job with the Metropolitan Opera in New York, which I am very pleased about. I encouraged him to go for the job, as I have lots of friends in New York, and I am going to go there eventually as well.

I will keep my job in the orchestra for at least a year, or until he is secure in his job, as he is still on trial, and I am commuting in the meantime with the baby who is fourteen months.

After Constantin left for America, most people were very sweet to the baby, but Constantin became a bit of a taboo subject for me. I felt some questions were very impertinent. People in the orchestra would ask me questions like, 'Is he still with his wife?' or, 'Do you ever see him?' I became rather offended by these sort of questions, because it wasn't genuine interest, or compassion, it was just plain, simple nosiness.

I don't think I handled it very well, and I used to get upset and not say anything. Maybe I was still quite emotional from having the baby.

Other orchestras are much more accepting of extra-marital relationships, but the LPO has always had the reputation of being rather prudish about that kind of thing. There was even once a phantom caller who used to phone up various wives and inform on people – there are always one or two relationships going on, particularly when the orchestra is on tour.

I don't have many friends in the orchestra. There are only two or three I spend time with, my desk partner Joe, Ishani in the first violins, although we don't have that much in common, and Joakim, who is, ironically, the new leader. Okay, he replaced Constantin, but that is not his fault. We get on very well.

The fact that I am friendly with Joakim, who is, I suppose, an eligible, single man, doesn't make me very popular with a lot of the women in the orchestra. I think they feel, oh, she's just nabbing the next leader again.

Joakim and I have actually discussed this. We don't want people to have the same worries they had when I was with Constantin, that they won't be able to talk to Joakim, so we take care we are not exclusively with each other. We are just good friends.

Richard Hosford
Co-principal Clarinet

'I have some horrendous dreams'

I HAD A TEACHER who was absolutely fanatical about cows. She just loved them, thought cows were wonderful, drew cows and sketched them, and when her performances were recorded, she insisted all her record sleeves had cows on the cover. She was a wonderful lady, but just slightly nutty.

When she discovered I was a farmer's son, she made every excuse to come down to the farm, so we would play clarinet to the cows. Because I was brought up on a dairy farm, I couldn't really see the romance in it. If anyone goes into a field of cows, and stays there long enough, they will come up and start licking you – but she thought this was absolutely wonderful, of course.

For the last ten years I was in the Chamber Orchestra of Europe, but there was always a longing to play in a symphony orchestra. Chamber orchestras are great, but there are only two or three Mozart symphonies with clarinets in them, and just three Mozart piano concertos – out of twenty-seven – so you are constantly left out of repertoire in chamber music.

The huge romantic repertoire, Tchaikovsky, Rachmaninov, and of course twentieth-century music, is where the best clarinet writing is. There is an enormous amount of wonderful music I didn't want to miss out on.

Tennstedt has obviously had an incredible relationship with

this orchestra, there is something quite special there. I have come in on what must be pretty much the end of it. He is always ill, so he often cancels. But he has got incredible performance charisma, and many symphonies are a real event.

His old-style German conducting where all the notes are sustained and there's not much articulation is quite out of date now, and it tends to lead to an incredibly slow tempo. I had the interesting experience of doing Beethoven 9 with him, having just recorded it with a chamber orchestra – it might well have been a different piece, it was at least half as long again. Under Tennstedt, the piece became a huge, vast monolith whereas, with the chamber orchestra, it was light and airy. There were good aspects to both, but it was extraordinary how different they could be.

At the moment, music is entirely my life. As a young guy, I worry that if I devote myself solely to playing the clarinet, I might regret not developing other interests along the way. Suppose I suddenly couldn't play any more? Or I got fed up with it? Or perhaps couldn't play as well as I used to? I mean, it happens to a lot of people. There is such a thing as too much music . . .

When the solos come up, people expect them to be right. There is not much room for error and that creates quite a lot of anxiety. I have some horrendous dreams of going on stage and not having the faintest idea what the first note is; or opening the clarinet case up five minutes before the concert, and I have forgotten to put it in when I left home. There are an awful lot of nights with anxiety dreams.

Nicola Hurton

First Violins

'If the performance is bad, everybody blames us; and if it's good, we don't get any thanks'

MY MOTHER DID push me quite a lot. I went to the Menuhin School to study violin when I was eleven, and stayed there until I was seventeen.

It was pretty ghastly. I wouldn't send my children to a place like that. It is a very small school, about thirty-five pupils, and I found that a bit cramping. It would have been nice to have mixed with more people my own age.

There was an awful pressure to do concerts, it was as if your whole sense of self-worth depended upon how many concerts you did. So you were always being judged on your playing, that was the most important thing, and I don't think they cared much about you as a person really. A lot of children there were very unhappy.

I used to get very nervous at concerts; I would shake a lot. I remember when I finally did a concert at which I thought I had played very well and felt I was beginning to get over the nerves. Menuhin came up to me afterwards; he didn't say anything about my playing, he just said, 'Now, about those bow shakes . . .' and proceeded to tell me what I could do to get rid of my bow shakes, which were a whole load of stupid exercises.

★　　　★　　　★

109

Nice as it is playing in the orchestra, when you are just channelled into music, you're not really using your brain anywhere else. The violin's a big part of my life, but it's not the only thing. So I'm studying psychology with the Open University, and that's very important to me.

If I get my degree I'd like to go on further. I'd be interested in how psychology could be applied to the orchestra, for instance motivating rank-and-file players. There's very little career structure in the orchestra for a rank-and-file player: you just sit there, and that's it for life, and you remain on the same money. It's a fairly thankless task.

I do feel unappreciated sometimes. Playing first violin, the music's really difficult, we've got loads more notes than anyone else. If the performance is bad, everybody blames us, and if it's good, we don't get any thanks.

I feel frustrated that we're always being told what to do. We have to go along with the conductor, and do what the leader says: there's very little room for us to feel we're putting anything of ourselves in, other than trying to play well.

Maybe that's one reason why I'm taking this psychology degree. With music, I sort of got pushed into it by my mother, whereas with this, I'm totally self-motivated. It has given me a bit of confidence, and a real sense of satisfaction, that I can do something for myself.

Russell Jordan
Timpani

'Most people notice the timpanist first . . .'

I'VE ALWAYS LIKED RHYTHM. As a child I enjoyed banging things, and I was always tapping – and getting told off for doing it. I've got some good rhythm in me, that's what it is, it's a kind of gift I guess.

I got it from my mum, who used to play the piano in a local pub in Leytonstone. She was a brilliant pianist by ear. Someone would call out a tune and she'd play it, no problem.

I went to a very rough East End school, where they didn't encourage music at all – I try to block out memories of that place, actually. If you were good at football and things like that then you were fine, anything like music or art was very much in the minority. I was the only one in the whole school who did music, so I was always an outsider. At one stage it nearly made me think, 'I can't go on with this, I'll give up completely.' Thank God I didn't. But it was an uphill battle the whole time, and it shouldn't have been: somebody with a talent like mine should have been encouraged.

When I was trying to get extra lessons before my college auditions, they tried to stop me. The headmaster actually said, 'We want you to do sport not music.'

Fortunately, I got into the Royal College of Music at fifteen. In fact, at that time I was the youngest person there.

★　　★　　★

III

Ever since I was very young, I've always wanted to play in the London Philharmonic, so it was fantastic when I got this job.

My favourite composers are the ones who write well for timpani. Richard Strauss, he's a wonderful writer for timpani. In *Salome*, there's one scene, the dance of the seven veils, where she takes off all her veils and does a sort of striptease on stage. That's fantastic timpani writing, a lot of different notes, and you play the bass line in some bits, which is quite advanced. At the end, there's a chromatic scale down from E natural, which is just incredible! But all Strauss's operas are full of things like that, they're so rewarding to play.

Janáček is another of my favourites. We're doing one of his pieces next season, Glagolitic Mass. That's incredible soloistic timpani writing, and wonderful to play.

Bruckner symphonies are like doing a work-out, they're incredibly physical. We did Bruckner's Fifth Symphony in Madrid the other night and, at the end of it, I was completely shattered.

Although we're way at the back, I think most people notice the timpanist first. You've got to be visible, but some guys in the profession do get carried away, and a timpanist can actually ruin performances by over-acting.

People who come to the LPO think I'm quite exciting to watch, but without being over the top.

John Kitchen

First Violins

'It is all too easy to get into bad habits'

MY FATHER WAS a violinist back in the 1920s, he played in the theatres at the old silent movies. When it was a Charlie Chaplin film, there were four or five of them playing in the pit. The cinemas were not plush as we know them today, they had wooden seats and loose gravel on the floor. On a Saturday afternoon, they used to flash the football scores on the screen, and if the local team had lost, they would put a wire mesh over the pit to stop all the eggs and tomatoes falling in.

He also played on the cruise liners, he was on the *Honoric*, which was the sister ship to the *Titanic*, playing in a little light orchestra for guests on board. He travelled the world on this ship, and had lots of stories about his travels.

During the Depression, he was unable to continue as a violinist, so he and my mother, who was a pianist, started a small curtain business, which was quite successful. But their great hope was to return one day to playing musical instruments.

My father is now ninety-three and he lives in a home in Lancaster, where he entertains everybody by telling them about the time he spent on the cruise line. We saw him recently. It was nice to see him looking so well, and I played the violin for him, and he criticized me, he said I should do some more practising.

★　　　★　　　★

I was aware of musical sounds from as long as I can remember, and my father introduced me to the violin when I was seven. It does need such a lot of concentrated dedication to put somebody on the right lines regarding them having a career as a musician. If your parents happen to be musical it helps enormously, not only in the practising, but just observing how things are going, intonation, style, and all the other essentials. Looking back, I am very pleased I had somebody who was strong enough to persuade me to practise a couple of hours a day.

There must always be a talent, but if there is a talent, then it helps if there is encouragement. In my case it started in a small way: playing at the local music festivals; I often came out with good results. I went to a Quaker school where there was a very great interest in music-making, and I was encouraged to play in the school orchestra. It was a good orchestra, and quite a lot of the people who were in it are now part of the profession.

When I was a young man, everybody was expected to do their National Service. In 1958 I went off to the Grenadier Guards' band. We played mostly light music, tunes from shows that were popular at the time, like *My Fair Lady*, and *King and I*. We often played outside Buckingham Palace in our red tunics, and we also played for the investitures, which were always on a Tuesday, I remember. Our job was to sit up in a little gallery, playing very discreetly, while the Queen was giving out her honours.

When my military service ended, I went into the BBC Symphony Orchestra. I was the youngest member, and everybody else seemed so old. I remember one lady of sixty who had spent the whole of her life with the BBC Symphony Orchestra, and I thought, my goodness, I don't think I will ever be that age. And now it is only a few years away for me . . . time goes so fast.

I joined the LPO more than a dozen years ago. It has changed tremendously, in fact, there are only three players in the first violin section who were here when I started.

We have had tremendous experience with Bernard Haitink,

and Klaus Tennstedt, and the Bruckner and Mahler symphonies. Those are two great conductors, with whom we all enjoyed working. But our principal conductor is Franz, and he is a very gifted, very talented young man. He has a style which is very much in the Viennese tradition, and he has a great selling quality to his music. He is going to have a great career – he has a great career at the moment, and it is going to go from strength to strength, I predict.

A piece I thoroughly enjoyed was the Schumann Spring Symphony which we did a fortnight ago, Franz conducted it with such flair and imagination. He is also a miraculous conductor of Bartók, which is a fiendishly difficult score. It demands the utmost concentration musically and intellectually, it is a score which has complex changes of key, and changes of expression and mood, and he was able to cope with that so clearly and so well, and still have a very relaxed state of mind after it, which is amazing.

Music is 100 per cent of my life, because the dedication to it doesn't allow much time for other things: it doesn't allow much time for hobbies, nor does it allow much time for social life. It doesn't, for example, allow for the Friday evening bash which people from other walks of life might have, nor a party on a Saturday night, because Sunday is not a free day. I often have to go to rehearsals on a Sunday. All the curtains are drawn in my street because people are sleeping late, and I am the first person to start up their car.

But I have a dedication to my profession, and I am very happy to do it. It is part of my temperament I suppose: I enjoy practising, I enjoy anything to do with the violin or to do with music.

Kathy Loynes
First Violins

'I don't like people looking at me . . .'

I AM FROM HARTLEPOOL in Cleveland, and left home at twelve to go to Cheetham's, which is a music boarding school; it was my decision, I wasn't pushed to go away.

It was a wonderful school, except I was terribly homesick. I was far too young to be separated from my parents, and I have regretted that ever since.

It is only now that I am beginning to realize what an effect it had on me. A personal relationship ended recently, and I actually had to investigate why I had so much sadness inside me. Even now, I become terribly choked up when I leave my parents, and that is not natural, it is not right, but I know it goes back to music school, and leaving home early.

When I have children, I will send them to one of the local music schools, and I don't care if it is not up to the standard of Cheetham's or the Menuhin School.

I went to the Guildhall School of Music because I won a scholarship. The standards were very low compared to my music school and I was very frustrated. I met people who could hardly get round the instrument, they had no basic technique, and nobody cared if you turned up to lectures or not. It felt as if there was too much freedom.

★ ★ ★

Right from the word go I knew that I belonged to the first fiddle section of the LPO, I loved their sound. I have played with most of the orchestras, but their attack and grit, that gutsy sound they produce, is the best.

Fairly recently, I have started going through a very anxious stage on the platform. Performing for an audience makes me very nervous. I don't like people looking at me, I would just rather not be the centre of attention. If I am on the outside, I worry I might drop my bow over the side of the stage – that is one of my greatest fears. There is a lot of stress involved, which manifests itself in bow shaking, palpitations, sickness, and I can hardly put the bow on the strings. It is at its worst in very soft piano passages.

The last movement for the first fiddles in Mahler 9 is notoriously pearly. There is one passage, the 'adagio', oh, it lasts for minutes and minutes, and it is all very, very soft, the bow is practically off the string, and I have great difficulty trying to control it.

Music is about 90 per cent of my life at the moment, which is not good. I would like more time to myself, I would like more social life. The problem is money; buying the flat and buying my fiddle all within a year didn't leave any money for a car, and I don't live in town, so getting around at night is not so good. Maybe in a year's time when the fiddle is paid for, and I am mobile again, then I will do less work and more socializing, and then I will be a bit happier.

I don't have much time for hobbies or interests, but I do enjoy something called Pilates, which is a method of exercise that is good for musicians. I have some lovely friends in Surrey who have children, and I spend quite a lot of time down there. I am interested in alternative medicines, Friends of the Earth, Greenpeace, and vegetarian cooking, all of that sort of thing, and I am a teetotaller as well.

As for relationships, I try to stay away from musicians, simply because you don't want to come home and talk shop, you already have it twelve hours a day, seven days a week, talking about repertoire and conductors, fee structure and tours. If you could choose, you'd go for somebody who is an opera lover or an amateur musician, because they'd have to have some understanding of music. There are only three single women in the orchestra, but I know my desk partner, Nicola, has the same attitude as me.

There are a lot of male chauvinist pigs around in this business, that's for sure. I remember when a friend of mine joined the orchestra. A certain gentleman in the second violins suggested that she might be better off staying at home, 'looking after her husband', and she is actually a very, very fine fiddle player – far better than he is.

When I was freelancing in the LSO, if a female soloist entered the room and she was pretty, the chaps would start knocking the backs of their instruments. The London Philharmonic has many more women than the LSO and we do the same to the chaps – if a gorgeous man walks in, we give them a taste of their own medicine. We won't be intimidated.

Roger Lunn
Cello

'They have magnificent locomotives in China . . .'

MY GRANDFATHER, whom I never knew, was a railwayman, he'd been a clerk on Waterloo Station. And my father used to take me, from when I was a baby, to the bridge over the railway at Surbiton, where we lived, to watch the trains go by. I'd see the expresses tearing by to Bournemouth, and the slow goods trains as well, and from a very early age, I would collect the numbers of the locomotives. So you see, railways are in my blood, and trains were, and still are, a great fascination to me.

My first music teacher was called Mrs Richardson, I used to have two lessons a week with her. She lived near Wimbledon Common, which meant my mother and I would catch a train. Of course, I loved the train ride, and at Wimbledon there was a goods yard, where I used to see the steam locos shunting. We would visit the Joe Lyons café by the station, which is no longer there, unfortunately, and I would have a fruit pie, an ice cream and a drink for tuppence in old money. That really started things off well for my cello lessons!

We would then get on a 93 bus, which took us up Wimbledon Hill, through the village, and let us off by Wimbledon Common, and we would walk half a mile down the road to Atherton Drive, where my teacher lived. She had a wonderful great house with highly polished floors, and I would sit on a pedestal, and play my cello.

When I was thirteen, I got a scholarship to King's School, Canterbury, and I had to say goodbye to my cello teacher in Wimbledon. She was very upset.

My parents didn't have a car – far too expensive – but of course the journey there by train was a great thing for me. We changed at Clapham Junction, which was very busy with trains everywhere, so I could take numbers, and at Waterloo the train to Canterbury would be pulled by a Battle of Britain class, or sometimes a D1, or the L1440, which was a clankety old thing.

In 1953, we had a big festival of music. The Queen Mother came to open a new hall at Canterbury and Benjamin Britten and Peter Pears gave recitals. I was given the job of turning over the pages for Benjamin Britten, which is marvellous to think about now, that I had such a privilege.

Another thing I remember in that same year: we had the great east-coast floods, which affected Kent tremendously, and one of my favourite little railways, the Canterbury & Whitstable Railway, which was built by Stevenson in 1830, had to reopen, to bring coal into Canterbury. It was splendid to see trains again on this funny little branch line.

My first job was at the Bournemouth Symphony Orchestra, and I used the Somerset & Dorset Railway quite a lot. I would ask the driver, 'Any chance of a ride?' and he'd say, 'Hop up, hop up, no one's looking . . .' And so I would go on this wonderful journey from Bournemouth to Bath. There are a lot of very steep hills on that line: you get to Evercreech Junction, and up the steep hill to Masbury Summit, and after that you come to Combedown Tunnel, and going uphill, the smoke was so incredible you couldn't see a thing, it was absolutely black, and stank like goodness-knows-what going through this tunnel. You'd come out the other end to a place called Midford, which is the most beautiful area of Somerset, and then there was the long climb down into Bath. It really was the greatest experience, and now you can't do it any more, they closed the line down in 1964.

In 1972, a place came open as number eight cello in the LPO, and I was invited to that position, and I have been there ever since.

My first tour with the LPO was China, and that was a really great tour. They have magnificent locomotives in China: enormous, howling monsters that are much much bigger than in Britain, although the railway gauge is the same.

When we toured Colombia, I went on a tremendous railway run from Bogotá to a place called Zipaquirá, and I was invited to go on the footplate of the locomotive. The hills were so steep they had to have two firemen in relay shovelling the coal in! And I was asked to drive and blow the whistle, and that was quite an experience, I can tell you.

Timetables are a special interest of mine as well – I can get anyone anywhere. I do get teased by people in the orchestra, they ask me how to get to Timbuktu, but I also get numerous serious questions about how to get here, there and everywhere, and sometimes I can do better than British Rail.

My wife and children think I am a nutcase. I would have loved my children to have been interested but, basically, they are not excited by trains.

I have a huge model railway up in the loft at home. It is nothing very special right now because it needs a little work on it, but you are welcome to come and have a look . . .

Joseph Maher

Second Violins

'That is when luck played its master stroke . . .'

DAD WORKED FOR Coras Iompar Eìreann, the national railway company of Ireland. He had been a famous hurling and football star in his day, and he was far more interested in sport than in music. But one of his brothers played piano and sang Nat-King-Cole style – I used to enjoy when he came to the house.

I was about seven when I started having music lessons. I was very keen on the violin. My parents weren't very clued into what was necessary to educate somebody musically, so they just found the nearest available teacher and sent me along. The lessons dragged on for many years, with grave frustrations because, basically, I had been sent to a piano teacher who dabbled in fiddle playing.

When I was in my teens, somebody at the Academy in Dublin realized I had a bit of talent, and they offered me a scholarship. Unfortunately, technically I was nowhere at that stage. In fact I got thrown out of the Academy by no less a man than Sidney Criller, who had been taken on as violin professor. He expected me to memorize the first movement of the Mendelssohn fiddle concerto in about two weeks, and I think his expectations were very unrealistic.

So I had to find a teacher. I went to the other main institution for music in Dublin, and Vanacek heard me play. 'Oh yes,' he said, 'you can play, but your hands are too big, you must play viola.' Fortunately, I was aware that he'd switched several people to viola, and I was no more interested in the viola than I was in trumpet, so I didn't take up his offer, he was no use to me.

That is when luck played its master stroke. I was introduced to the director of the college of music in Limerick, and he listened to me play, and he said, 'Well, if you want, you can come and study with me.' Limerick is 120 miles away from Dublin, but because my father worked on the railway, we were entitled to free passes, so I went once a fortnight, and within a year I was working as a professional.

After I had done ten years in Liverpool as number five first fiddle, everything seemed a bit static, and I began to get the feeling I was being taken for granted. So I decided it was time to make a move. I wanted to know what it was like to work in London, and I knew if I never tried, I would be on my death bed thinking, that was something I should have gone for . . .

You have outstanding players in provincial orchestras, but there are not enough of them, and you never get amazing highs because they don't have the conductors. In a nutshell, there is a much higher standard in London, it is as simple as that.

Well, playing with the LPO was incredibly exhilarating. The consistently high standards through the sections impressed me most of all, plus the sound they made, the wall-of-sound sensation, really bowled me over, it was overwhelming, actually.

I have played in the second violins now for a number of years and, quite bluntly, I would like to be back playing first.

The only thing I can do is start to work my playing up, so that I can do a good audition, and see what they say. Positions are coming up, but it will take me a year to get where I want to be. At this stage, it is going to be a difficult task to switch, and I would need to play very well to make it clear that I am the right material.

It has been a long road for me. Okay, I started when I was seven, but in terms of moving forward and learning, I was nearly seventeen before that happened, so I lost those ten years at the beginning, I was kind of robbed of them. Had I gone to a very good teacher when I was seven, it might have turned out quite differently for me. That is conjecture, and you can't live in the past, but it does occur to me every so often.

Rachel Masters

Principal Harp

'I have very strong hands'

WHEN I WAS LITTLE, I was fascinated by the egg-slicer in the kitchen. It had ten wires on it, just like harp strings, which you pulled down over the egg, and I used to plink these wires all the time.

I nagged my parents for a couple of years about playing the harp, and because I didn't stop nagging, eventually, my mother tracked down a teacher.

The first time I touched the harp, I put it on the wrong shoulder – it goes on the right shoulder, and I put it on the left.

I know everybody says their instrument is the hardest, but it is a very demanding instrument, not least because it weighs about a hundredweight with its cover on, and you've got to have a house and a car which it can fit into.

I've got an estate car and it lies down in the back of that, and I've got a trolley, like a golf trolley, so I can move it myself, so long as there are no stairs – and then you've just got to get somebody to help you. There's a guy called Dougie who shifts harps and percussion around London. I suppose you'd call him a freelance shifter, and he will take a harp to an airport, bring it home for me, whatever.

People always want to know how much a harp costs. Mine's worth about £14,000, which is not that much actually, you can spend twice that. But they never cost a great deal, because they don't improve with age like violins, there's a lot of tension on the overall frame, and eventually the wood warps, and the mechanism loses its accuracy.

The harp is first mentioned in the Bible. Then they were little lap harps two or three feet high, with ten strings. Gradually, it developed the belly and the soundboard, and a curvy top.

There are forty-seven strings on a full-size modern harp, which is six and a half octaves, just a little bit less than the range of a piano. The modern design is bigger, more buxom, and stronger, designed to be moved around and withstand the rigours of late twentieth-century life – and Dougie!

When you pluck the strings, you don't use your little fingers, you only use three fingers and a thumb, and you're pulling your fingers into the palms of your hands in a sort of cupping action. It takes years to build up a good strength and suppleness in your fingers, I've got hundreds of technical exercises which I've used. I have very strong hands, I'm good at undoing tight bottle tops.

The harp is considered very romantic, somehow. People think: Oh, harps, how lovely, pretty women in beautiful long dresses with flowing hair, and angels . . . all this crap. I get fed up with that image of it. Sure, if you do a harp glissando, or rolled chords, it is a very luscious, warm sound, but the harp can be a very stark, terse instrument as well. It's very good for twentieth-century music, Benjamin Britten, Stravinsky, Prokofiev, and a lot of the avant-garde modern stuff as well.

If you have a great conductor, he can inspire and lift a perform-ance into something memorable. Zubin Mehta is a joy to play for. He is very musical, as though he feels the music coming through his body, and it's just obvious what he wants from us.

But there are very few that are very good, and an awful lot of conductors who are lousy. You'd be surprised how few con-ductors can actually give you a good, clear beat, and if you have somebody on the box who is not clear, it's difficult to know where to put the notes and, immediately, you feel less confident.

I have to tell you, I don't like conductors as people. A lot of them are very destructive, they can ruin people's careers. I've been intimidated on numerous occasions. One conductor, in particular, gave me a hell of a roasting recently. It was the first rehearsal of a very difficult violin concerto, and he kept on stopping the orchestra and commenting on things I was doing wrong, which I thought, seeing it was the first rehearsal, was rather unnecessary. At one stage he said, in front of everyone, 'You really should look at your music in advance, that harmonic's in the wrong octave.'

You have to take all this, it's like if you serve in a shop, the customer is always right – the conductor is always right. But I didn't like that. He really rattled me.

I went up to him during the break, and I said, 'I *have* looked at this in advance, and I want to get this right as much as you do . . .' He apologized.

Unfortunately, I was so rattled by that experience, that in the concert I came in six bars early. It's the worst thing I've ever done, the biggest, crassest, most ghastly mistake I have made, and I hope it doesn't happen again for an awfully long time.

But he made me do that, because he really shook my self-confidence. He can go away and conduct another concert, knowing it wasn't him who made that mistake. But, as all musicians know, you are only as good as your last performance, and when your confidence goes, it's very hard for you to do your job.

The older generation of maestro hate seeing women in principal seats, and this conductor has given other women a hard time.

There are quite a lot of men in the orchestra who don't like to think of women as intelligent people who can express themselves articulately. In some ways, symphony orchestras are the last bastion of male chauvinism, and I do think women in prominent seats get more flack than they deserve.

Anne McInerny
Trumpet

'Isn't it a man's instrument . . . ?'

I WAS BROUGHT UP in the Shankhill Road in Belfast. We stayed
there until the troubles were fairly lively, and then we moved
out to Bangor, which is a little seaside resort. We had a little
corner shop which sold general groceries and sweets.

At Bangor Girls High School, there were three or four girls
who could play brass instruments. The music teacher shoved a
trombone in my hands, which I didn't like at all, and eventually
I was given a trumpet.

Right from the start I was attached to it. On my grade VIII
report, the examiner wrote on the bottom, 'you obviously love
playing this instrument . . .' and he wished me good luck for
the future, which was very nice.

Music is my life, totally my life. Apart from playing, I am
interested in music from an academic perspective as well and I
am doing a Masters degree. I often bring the work into the Hall.
I found that in rehearsals you have got so much time hanging
around doing nothing, especially us brass players, because we
don't play in every movement, that I felt, rather than reading
some junk novel, I would put the time to good use. When I am
not playing, I am reading and writing about music.

People are always quite surprised to come across a woman
brass player. They ask, 'Why do I want to play the trumpet
when I am a woman?' or, 'Isn't it a man's instrument?' But

musicians come in all shapes and sizes, and I don't think sex is relevant really.

I spend a lot of time with men, I get on very well with them, I am a bit of a tomboy at heart but, occasionally, it would be nice to have a few more women around. Going out with the boys from the brass section, especially on tour, can be very boisterous.

There are a couple of women in the orchestra I go round with on tour. Rachel, the percussionist, is a woman in a man's world as well, she's a nice lassie, and there is another girl I'm friendly with, Jo St Leon from the viola section, who's great company too, and we'll have a couple of glasses of wine and a good chat.

I've recently had problems with my teeth. I had some crowns in front, and one decided it didn't want to be there any more. To fix that, I had to have three teeth taken away and a bridge put in. As you can imagine, it is very risky for a brass player to have something that major done on the front of the mouth, as the shape of your teeth define your *embouchure*.

I took four days off and had a change of *embouchure* and, after I had the teeth fixed, I had to retrain the muscles. It was like learning to walk all over again. For the next concert, they very kindly put me on the fifth trumpet chair in Mahler 1, which means all I had to do was come in at 57/157 in the last movement. That was great because I thought, yes, I can do this. If I hadn't been able to do that small part, my confidence would have been greatly shaken.

Gareth Mollison
French Horn

'Eight out of ten blocked drains are caused by cooking fat being poured down them'

MY PARENTS OFTEN took us to concerts at the Festival Hall, particularly the London Philharmonic as it happened. Nick Busch was first horn then, and I can distinctly remember the first time I heard him, he played Stravinsky's *Pulchinella*. He had a remarkable influence on my musical life as a matter of fact. All through school Nick was my idol as a horn player, so it was like a dream to get in the LPO. And it's pretty strange I'm sitting next to him now.

The National Youth Orchestra was good fun. They had a double horn section, and two friends and I were in the front section. Chris, Phillip, and me: it seemed like we were indestructible. The three of us were always together, we were going to share a flat. We were very supportive of each other, which helped our playing, and we had competitions to see how long we could practise – we once did five hours, which is unbelievable.

And then Chris drowned on a canoeing holiday in Scotland. I had been planning to go, but I couldn't be there at the last moment because of a rehearsal. Otherwise I might have drowned with him, as I can't swim.

Because he died, I stayed at home a lot, whereas I would have done a lot of horn practice with him pushing me, because that's what he was like. He was very encouraging and a very fine player, in fact, I don't know anyone who was as good as him, so it is a shame he died really.

That event changed my life considerably, in all sorts of strange ways.

There was a girl Chris had just started going with. Because he wasn't around, I looked after her a lot and, eventually, got involved with her, which was more for him than me I think.

From the Academy I went to Iceland for two seasons, and played with the Iceland Symphony Orchestra. At that time Ashkenazy was connected with the orchestra, and he would get his friends over, like Perlman and Rostropovich.

The Icelanders are a bit crazy. Every night, there would be a party and everybody would sit with a bottle in front of them. I've never again seen drinking like that. I had an Icelandic girlfriend or two. They are as beautiful as everyone says, and they're very free on the sexual front – not that I took advantage – but the guy I lived with, who was a bass player . . . it was a different girl each weekend. Unbelievable!

And then a job in the LPO came up, so I phoned Nick Busch and asked if I could do a trial. I got the job.

The worst parts are the stress, getting nervous and feeling you have to play when you're not in the mood, or you don't feel you're going to make a good job of it. Stage fright happens quite a lot, I get upset stomach or diarrhoea before a concert.

We did *Fidelio* last night. The opening has these horn bits, and they're very exposed, and they can go wrong . . . I woke up feeling nervous and worried, there was real anxiety until I'd done it. Luckily, it went very well.

The worst moment for me recently was Haydn's *Trauer* Symphony. There's a high second-horn part, and we performed it three times, and each time I messed up. That came at a time when the orchestra was very busy, and all the performances came after rehearsal for something else, and I didn't have the strength in my lip to play a high part.

There are times when work seems to be never-ending, and

your playing suffers. In Germany and America, they're funded properly, and they don't have to work the way we do. In the Berlin Phil. for example, there are ten horns, and they do half the work we do, so they have time to practise and to have fresh lips.

I like to invent things in my spare time.

One invention has just gone on the market, it's called Menu Mates, which is a translation aid. I had the idea when we were in Japan on tour. It has pictures of food, so that if you go into a foreign restaurant and you can't speak the language and read the menu, you can pull this thing out, and it's got pictures you or the waiter can point to.

I also designed a board game about pop music, and a thing called The Fat-Trap which is for used cooking fat: did you know eight out of ten blocked drains are caused by cooking fat being poured down them?

I could remain in the orchestra until I drop, which seems to be what happens to musicians, particularly on the horn. Or I could get lucky with an invention, and find an easy way out. I'd rather get lucky with an invention.

Sarah Newbold

Piccolo

'I suppose it is a bit odd to play the piccolo'

FOR SOME REASON, I decided when I was thirteen that I was going to be a professional flute player. God knows why, there was no real rhyme or reason, because I had never heard a professional orchestra, and I didn't hear one until I was eighteen.

That first time was amazing, it was such a huge sound, and I was fascinated by the number of people that get together to do it.

I played flute at school, but there was a girl in my year who had been playing longer than me, so I had to play the piccolo.

It used to be considered that the flute had the glamour, and the piccolo was something you did if you failed as a flute player, partly because it hasn't got much music written for it in solo repertoire. But you can play the piccolo with as much sonority and passion as you can the flute. The piccolo plays all the notes the flute does, except it doesn't go down to C and C sharp at the bottom, D is its lowest note.

The piccolo can have lots of different sounds. It has a bright, brilliant quality at the top of something, but it can also make a very lonely, desolate sound, as in a lot of Shostakovich – he wrote brilliantly for the piccolo and all the freaky instruments, like the tuba.

We did Shostakovich 10 the other night, and it was magical. I had never done that piece before, and it has a huge, rather frightening solo at the end of the first movement. As the music starts to die down, there is this piccolo duet, which then peters out into one piccolo, with the cellos and basses being left at the end, and you are stuck on these long notes, very, very quietly, just slowing everything down, and fading away . . .

Usually, I get nervous about a performance three or four days before, and wonder why on earth I am doing this – I must be mad! I get bad tempered, and feel like hiding under the duvet and never coming out again. Also, I have awful anxiety dreams. My most common is that the curtains open, and I am alone on the stage, and I don't even know which concert we are playing. Fortunately, I usually wake up at that point.

A social life is difficult for anyone in this business because we are away such a lot, and the hours are terrible. It is very hard to do other things, but I am learning to tap dance, which is great fun. I love the music that goes with it, songs like 'Leaning on a Lamp Post', and Gershwin-type things.

We've learned to do shuffles, shuffle-ball-change, shuffle hops and step hops, you can start stringing them together pretty quickly. It is actually quite hard work for my brain trying to remember which way to go. I am very good at going right, but I can't seem to get the hang of going left. At night, I do my homework in the kitchen, although there's not a lot of room!

I am single. It would be great not to go out only with musicians but, practically speaking, you have to eliminate anyone who works regular nine-to-five hours. We are often working until ten or eleven at night and, inevitably, sleep late in the morning.

Also, non-musicians often can't understand the stresses involved, and why I get nervous. Nor the highs. After a concert that goes well, you're feeling such relief to have survived it, or maybe you've actually enjoyed the performance, and all this tends to make you over-excited. You have a drink with the other musicians after the concert and hold a post-mortem, and maybe they're also on a high . . . and the other person can feel very excluded.

My mother and sisters came to the concert last night because I was doing a solo. I know they are proud, but they're always saying, it's a funny old thing I do. And I suppose it is a bit odd to play the piccolo.

Leo Phillips

First Violins

'I was dirty and smelly and generally disliked'

I COME FROM quite an arty background: my mother describes herself as a failed pianist; my father's a painter. They thrust a violin under my chin at an early age; they maintain they weren't ambitious, but I felt the weight of their ambition behind me.

I went to Dulwich College because I was awarded the full music scholarship – that was one of the few things in life I aimed at and got, thank goodness, because my parents wouldn't have been able to afford to send me there otherwise. My sister, meanwhile, had gone to the Menuhin School, and she was asked if she knew anyone who played as well as her, and she suggested me.

So I left Dulwich College after a year to go to the Menuhin School, and it was an unmitigated disaster.

A school with so few people, ages ranging from eight to eighteen, in the middle of nowhere, is quite limiting. The socializing influence of having two hundred boys your own age around you was lost when I left Dulwich, and it would have done me a lot of good.

Precocious, musical children are very volatile, difficult people, and I felt the teachers, certainly when I was there, did not know how to handle difficult children, no matter how good their intentions were. A number of people I was at that school with have gone through enormous traumas, and many have given up music.

143

I've actually blacked out a lot of this period, but it was a really miserable time; my parents were having problems, as well, so there was no stability from that end.

Menuhin turned up very rarely, and dithered around. He didn't seem to know what was going on really, I had about five minutes with him.

I was the stroppiest person in the world. I didn't do any work, and I had absolutely no discipline, I was dirty and smelly and generally disliked. I was considered sufficiently anti-social to be given a room by myself, which could be deemed a luxury, but was meant to be a punishment, and it felt like a punishment.

I didn't do any work. I had enough talent to be able to get by without doing any, but it was a party trick, something I could do, like other people can play football or paint. And I wasn't interested in music anyway. I wasn't passionate about it until much much later.

The first piece that really got me going was the Schubert Quintet and, later, Mozart 39, after which I was absolutely hooked: one of the chords in the introduction of 39 is a C minor with a D flat, and the power of that chord just sent me. Mozart 29 is beautiful too, quite incredible. When you first really listen to a Mozart symphony, which I hadn't done, it's unbelievably exciting.

I'm still very lazy, and I don't go out of my way to hear music which is new to me, but if I stumble across something and like it, I'm more enthusiastic than anyone.

We've just done Janáček's Glagolitic Mass, and that was really amazing. I like things that are loud and fast, I still haven't grown out of that. In that work you have to pitch notes you aren't used to, its intervals are very strange, technically it's extremely difficult to play. But the orchestra played it magnificently, they really responded to the conductor, and they nailed it.

People are so receptive in the LPO, there's more warmth in this orchestra than in any other I've come across, and they put more of themselves into the music than any other band.

★   ★   ★

Music is absolutely vital to me, I couldn't live without it. I listen to it all the time, I have it on in the flat, or if I'm walking down the road. I've always got music going in my head, it's the most important thing in my life.

But I hate being thought of as a musician. I'm a human being, and I think that's more important. I don't want people to make assumptions as to my character, or my possible reactions to anything, based on the fact that I'm a musician. We shouldn't be categorized like that.

People assume we're serious, a bit woolly, a bit girly perhaps, but that's no more sophisticated than being seen at primary school with a violin case and immediately branded a cissy.

It's nice to talk about music, but there's more to life than music. I constantly worry that a lot of musicians, myself included, often do not see that clearly enough.

Robert Pool
First Violins

'There are three of us who are gay in the orchestra . . .'

MY MOTHER . . . I rang her last night and asked how old I was when I started. She put me on the piano at six – I was absolutely hopeless – and then I began violin, which she taught me for the first year.

Every day, she pushed me to rehearse. Because I am very sweet-toothed, I was bribed, I can still see the packets of jelly beans downstairs in the hallway, which I'd come and get after I had done my practice.

After that, I went to a local teacher, Miss Wilmot-Smith. My mother insisted she sit in for the lessons, until she was banned for interrupting, and would then have to wait in the kitchen. I loathed the teacher, she was hard and demanding, and would say horrible things about my playing. I used to leave the lessons crying.

For years I went to these violin lessons – I did everything my mother asked of me. She was quite strong, suffocating, I would say. I had no ambitions of my own. I never pushed myself as a child, never made a conscious decision that I wanted to be an orchestral musician. Having lessons, going to college – they were all mother's ideas.

I never thought I had talent, I still don't to be honest. I often think I'd like to do something else, particularly on a bad day, like the other day when the conductor wanted to hear me play alone, and I completely went to pieces.

147

It was just a section rehearsal of a modern piece, but when he called on me I was so nervous, I couldn't play, and it ruined the day. Then, when we did it all together, I could play it perfectly. If I'd known I was going to be called on, maybe I'd have had a betablocker before, and I'd have been fine.

All musicians find ways to combat nerves. Betablockers are meant for people with a heart condition, they slow your heart down if it starts over-beating. I take them if I know there's going to be something very slow and exposed at a big concert, sometimes I take half of one, and that just takes the edge off the nerves. It has no other physical effect, except I tend to sweat a little bit more. There are some people who take pills for every single rehearsal and every single concert. Some people go to psychiatrists.

I did when I was younger, my mother made me go. I was eighteen, just starting college, and my mum found out I was gay. She had been going through my wallet and found somebody's name and phone number, and put two and two together. I could have denied it, but I didn't.

Of course, she went completely mad. Her biggest concern was that people would find out: 'My God, what will the neighbours think?' which was stupid, I didn't give a damn what they thought and she didn't even like them. But that's what she worried about, and she took to her bed for weeks.

Then she made me see a psychiatrist. It cost a fortune and my mum had to go out to work to pay for it, which she loathed because she hates being with other people. In fact, both my parents are reclusive, they only come out to Festival Hall concerts.

After college I went to Germany, which was probably the best thing I ever did in my life – my mum encouraged me. I was there for three years and that, I suppose, was when I was at my happiest.

I was desperately homesick at first, I didn't speak German, and I didn't talk to anyone for months. But, after a while, I met an American chap, and then an English girl, and gradually I got to know a whole circle.

People knew I was gay, but I was accepted, and I felt at ease with it. Germany was quite an accepting place in those times, it's changed now, sadly.

When my money began to run out, I started to play in a chamber orchestra. That was fun at first, but there were some fabulous players there, and I felt I wasn't good enough.

I always think I'm not good enough. Sometimes, I sit in the orchestra and I can hear people struggling around me not being able to play something I can play and I'll think, well, maybe I'm not all that bad . . . But, generally, I sit through rehearsal and my hands are cold from the minute I have the violin in my hand. As soon as rehearsal's over, my hands warm up. Maybe I should see the psychiatrist again.

My first orchestral job in England was with the BBC Symphony, and after a few years, I auditioned for a position in the LPO.

Being in the LPO felt grown up after the BBC, which is a bit of a backwater – the only excitement you ever got there was the Last Night of the Proms.

I'll never forget the first concert I did with the LPO. It was with Klaus Tennstedt and I couldn't believe the noise people made, everyone going hell for leather. In the Beeb, everything was a bit timid, rather straight-laced, and no one was terribly bothered. The difference was amazing.

I like working for Klaus, I always enjoy his concerts. But he's cancelling a lot of dates now, and we don't seem to be getting the top names conducting us. The orchestra's in a mess, which is sad. I feel very stressed about it all. I wake up at nights sweating and anxious. Will the orchestra be here next year? Only a year ago we were riding high, it's extraordinary how quickly fortunes can change.

I'm forty this July. I do wonder what I'm going to be doing in ten years' time. I mean, being gay, I'm not 100 per cent sure about my status. I worry about my health a lot, and in many ways I have reason to, having looked after someone who was terminally ill: my boyfriend died a year ago.

There are three of us who are gay in the orchestra. I have very little to do with them, I'm wary of them. But there's a gay cello extra who's a friend of mine, and we go out to gay clubs a lot on tour.

I'm not in a relationship now. When the last one finished, I found it easier being alone. Besides, the relationships I've had have always been with people where I've been the provider, I've been the one looking after them, which is exhausting. I suppose that goes back to my mother, it's because of my mother doing everything for me that I want to do it for someone else. But it's so stupid, I'm just carrying on a chain which isn't being broken, and I hate myself for it.

What's nice about our section is that we have a good time together. If you look at the cellos and the violas, they are all sitting there looking miserable, but even when there's some horrendous session we always have a good time in the violins, we play jokes on each other, do outrageous things.

The girls tease me a lot. We did a tour of Europe, and they sent ahead made-up letters, supposedly from my mother, to every single hotel. When we arrived in Amsterdam, there was this huge parcel, a 'safe-sex kit', which had tissues and condoms. Then a telegram was waiting in Munich: 'Dear, darling Robbsy, I've found these strange magazines under your bed, what does it all mean?'

There's something coming up which is going to be great. It's Katherine Loynes' thirtieth birthday, and we've got a photograph of her naked in the jacuzzi – with strategic bubbles – which Nicola took when they shared a room on tour. We're going to send it around the whole orchestra, and everyone will sign it, and when it gets passed back to her . . . I can't wait.

Not everybody in the section is part of the fun and games; there's a whole new bunch of young people in the front. They're very serious and probably think we're awfully childish. The young ones coming in nowadays seem frighteningly conscientious. They don't drink, and they don't seem to let their hair down – there's no spark, which is a shame.

There are a few left who behave disgracefully. I remember an Italian tour where we had what was called a towel party, and you could only come if you put your towels to good use. So there were togas, and head scarves, and I remember one of the violas came with a bra on his head for some reason – it was outrageous.

With regard to my mother, she's never said anything, but I know she hoped I'd be better than an orchestral musician, that I would be a soloist or something, but she's now realized it isn't going to happen.

Geoffrey Price
Second Violins

'I don't see our role as secondary to the first violins'

WE WERE QUITE a musical family. My parents played the piano and everybody sang and, being Welsh, we all reckoned we could sing very well.

When I was about eight or nine, my friend was having violin lessons, and I said, 'Oh, can I see your violin?' I had never held a violin before, and I picked out the notes, bow as well, of 'Half a Pound of Tuppeny Rice'. In fact, it is quite easy to do, open string, second finger, fourth finger – and then you have to fiddle to get the top note. But it was all there, and I said to my parents, 'I quite like that . . .'

At school, the music master came round: 'Here are some violins, anybody want to learn?' I put up my hand. It was a Stradivarius – just joking – but it was a smashing little fiddle, and I started lessons with the teacher. After about a month, I started going to him privately, and by the end of that term, I had got into the Swansea Youth Orchestra. I gave up playing rugby because the old hands were getting trampled on, and I was really more keen on music by this time.

That summer, I auditioned for the National Youth Orchestra of Wales, and I got in. Then I decided the best thing was to come to London. My parents said, 'Well, that is fine, as long as you get a scholarship' – money being not that plentiful.

I played for a scholarship at the Guildhall, which I got, and my teacher there was a Viennese chap. You simply didn't get past the second note if everything wasn't absolutely perfect, posture, bow control, bow pressure and, most of all, intonation. Consequently, it took ages and ages to get through a piece, or even a study or a scale – dear God, it was awful. But there was a method in his madness: because he was so critical of everything you did, if you ever did get round to playing anything, it was pretty good. I managed to stick him for three years, and I am very glad I did, because I would have become lazy had I not had somebody like him chasing the life out of me.

I played around with the girls a lot, which used to irritate him. He would say, 'Would you kindly exercise your fingers on the violin just once in a while.'

I don't see our role as secondary to the first violins. Sure, they are the ones right on the top, but they need our wonderful sound just underneath them, otherwise they sound thin and wiry. We're not so much an inner voice as, say, the violas.

My instrument is an unnamed Neapolitan violin. It has been a bit battered, but it is a wonderful fiddle, and I know its foibles – for instance, it doesn't like the damp weather, it sounded awful this morning – and I know how to treat it, and it never lets me down. It has done me very proud over the years.

I've always liked playing with Klaus very much. Some conductors have got a wonderful technique, very clear, cerebral, but no soul, no music. Klaus's enthusiasm and dedication to what he is doing, a genuine love for the music he is performing, shows in his body as much as his face, he has a vitality and vibrance that is just amazing.

My wife and the children come first, but I have to say, there couldn't be life without music. I love going to work, they are a great bunch of people in the LPO, a very friendly lot.

I intend to stay with the London Philharmonic, and I want to be at the front as long as possible. I have been lucky with the back and the neck and the shoulders, and if you sit correctly when you play, you can minimize those wearing-out effects.

Moving back would be for my last few years, but for the moment, I am as fit as an orchestral player ever is.

Well, that is basically it. I love playing, and I am very lucky to be doing something I want to do. I wanted to play the violin in an orchestra, and there is nothing better, it's wonderful!

John Price
Principal Bassoon

'The audience stood up and cheered'

MY FATHER WAS a jazzer in Tommy Dorsey's swing band before the war. When he came back home, there was no work, and he had a wife and family to support. As he had trained as an engineer in the army, he went straight into engineering, and gave up his music career.

Each evening when he came in from work, he used to make me practise for half an hour. Of course, at the age of nine all I wanted to do was to play cowboys and Indians, and I can remember tears streaming down my face, not wanting to do it, and him saying, 'No, half an hour's practice . . .' I'm grateful now.

I was in the RPO for ten years, and then a vacancy came up in the LPO, and they asked if I would like to join them. I have now been in the orchestra for sixteen years.

One beautiful girl joined within a few months of me, she was in the first violin section. I noticed her immediately, and I thought, my goodness . . . if I hadn't gone from the RPO to the LPO, I would never have met my wife.

It is wonderful when Tennstedt conducts because he always draws out of you more than you think you have to give. Take Bruckner 4 in Vienna, I mean, *that* was a performance. Even the critics said in the papers the next day, 'It takes an English

157

orchestra to come here to show us how to play Bruckner.' The Musickwerein, which is the Vienna Philharmonic's hall, is a magnificent place, with wonderful acoustics. Of course, there's a lot of pressure on any visiting orchestra to play well there because of the tradition it has got. But as soon as Tennstedt walked on to the platform, we knew something special was going to happen.

This particular Bruckner symphony starts off very quietly with the strings. Then the principal horn comes in with a solo, very soft, but very high, and he keeps repeating this phrase until he gets to a tremendous climax. One is always a little bit apprehensive at this point, because the horn solo is so difficult, but our principal horn played it absolutely magnificently.

The reaction once we had finished was amazing, the audience stood up and cheered – and we repeated it the next night, and it was even better! That was all down to Tennstedt. Certainly, the musicians have got to produce the goods, but you need somebody like him to get it out of you.

Unfortunately, all the great conductors are dying off now. Haitink is as strong as an ox, I hope I am as healthy as he is when I get to his age. But Klaus is very ill, I can't think we are going to do many more concerts with him. He is very much slower, his voice is husky with the cancer he had. He has problems walking now, sometimes his skin colour is very strange, and he has problems with his eyes, and dizziness. He is not a well man . . .

There is so much work in this job, that you can't really enjoy the music because you are tired. Of course, you are going to do your very best, and it will be a good performance, no doubt about that, but it won't be as sparkling as it should be because you are walking on to the platform tired.

If you compare our workload to that of an American orchestra, or even a major European orchestra, there is no comparison, we work three to four times more. We often work a couple of months without a day off – and we probably earn half what they get. It's not fair, is it?

Martin Robertson

Saxophone

'It's quite a wild beast . . .'

I TOOK UP CLARINET at school, and one day the teacher said, 'Do you fancy doing some saxophone, because we've got a position in the band?' So he gave me a saxophone, and that was it, I loved it, and I played both clarinet and saxophone from the age of eleven.

To start with they're quite similar but the more specialized you get, the more difficult it is to keep them both going. There's a completely different way of blowing, the resistance and the fingering is different as well.

When I was fifteen, my grandmother gave me the money for a saxophone, which is still the nicest saxophone I've ever played, it was a Selmer Super 1945. They are actually very rare and difficult to get hold of. This one was owned by the lead alto saxophonist in the Ivy Benson Band, which was an all-female British jazz band in the 1940s and 1950s.

What happened was this: the woman retired and went to Australia, she couldn't take the saxophone with her – maybe she had too much luggage, so she gave it to a little boy (I don't know what his relationship was with her), who decided he didn't want to play it. His family advertised it in *Exchange & Mart*, and I went and bought it for £140. When I got it, it still had the original mouthpiece, with a lipstick stain all around it.

★　　　★　　　★

It's funny, when you're a child you just do things without thinking about it. My music teacher used to say: 'You're going to go to the Royal College of Music,' and I would think, 'Oh, am I? Great.'

At the Royal College of Music there were only about two or three saxophonists, which in some ways was good because it meant that I had plenty of stuff to do, but on the other hand, there weren't enough of us to have a quartet. Now they have two quartets at the Royal College because the saxophone is growing in popularity all the time, and more and more modern composers are using it in orchestras.

Funnily enough, it's the anniversary of the saxophone this year, it's been around for 150 years.

You can actually change the sax's sound a lot, which gives it a great freedom of expression. It's so versatile, lots of music suits it. For instance, with a soprano saxophone you can get a pretty good cor anglais sound, very attractive, very mellow, but much more powerful.

Alto saxes are more French horn orientated, and if you play jazz or rock, you can change the sound completely and make it much more razor-edged and punchy. It's an incredible jazz instrument! Also, different types of mouthpieces enable the instrument to play different sounds, shallower, higher, tighter, harder, brighter . . .

It is a very loud instrument. Usually, we're sat behind the flutes in an orchestra, and the flutes dread having us there, because they know we're going to be loud. Also, I know they feel the saxophone can be pretty coarse sometimes, and it's true that the saxophone can sound a little crude compared to the compactness of other wind instruments – it's quite a wild beast.

When I'm really going for it, and enjoying myself, it's a very powerful experience, your whole body works towards producing the sound, and it comes from right inside, and deep down. That is a wonderful feeling, it's so exciting. It's quite a sexy instrument to play, and I do sometimes think about naughty things when I play.

I've worked with all the orchestras now, and they're all completely different, but the LPO, when it performs, can be the most animal. They seem to have a certain anger behind their playing which is very exciting. Like any orchestra, if they have a conductor they respect, then they really pull their fingers out. I've done quite a lot of Mahler with Tennstedt, and that's always a wonderful show because they love playing for Tennstedt, there's something about him that draws them out. He's quite an angry guy himself in a way, and he feeds it to them, and they chuck it back in his face.

Music is my life. I can't imagine being without it, I listen to music if I'm not playing it, I have it going through my head all the time. I don't think you can have too much music: it's such a healing thing, it's so good for you . . .

I'm mad about cooking – I would be a chef if I wasn't a musician. Well, it's creative, isn't it? And I need to create all the time. Anything, you name it, I could do it for you. I like all the Oriental stuff – Thai, Chinese, Vietnamese, Malaysian – and all the differences in between. I'm into French, both country type French-style cooking, and the great, poncey stuff.

I've got all the recipe books by all the up-and-coming chefs, I'm fascinated by what they're doing. They're all very different, they're like soloists. You have people like Marco Pierre White, who is an arrogant sod, but very talented, a fantastic chef, his work is just ingenious. And then Anton Mosimann is brilliant, but completely different, he's very Swiss, and neat and tidy, but absolutely wonderful.

I dream about music all the time. Either they can be insecurity dreams, where you're standing on stage with nothing on or, sometimes, I compose things and I have the tunes in my head when I wake up.

I'd love to have more time to write music, but once you're doing mortgages and kids, you've got to earn money, and sitting down and writing music takes time . . . but I'm hoping that will happen eventually.

Kevin Rundell
Principal Bass

'We are underpinning everything . . .'

MY GREAT-GRANDFATHER was a founder member of the LSO. His son, who was my mother's father, was Sir Thomas Beecham's principal in the late 1940s. He was a bass player. I can remember visiting him when we were young. We were always told, 'you must never touch the bass' – my mother had obviously had the life scared out of her when she was a kid. I remember looking at it and thinking, it can't be that hard, and I said to him, 'Will you show me how it works?' He was delighted. He was quite old then, and the question of what he was going to do with this instrument must have gone through his mind. He gave me my first lesson then and there, he taught me a scale, and every Saturday after that he would come over and give me a bass lesson.

We spent a lot of time together, just the two of us, and I became very close to my grandfather. I think he felt it his mission to pass on everything he knew. Orchestras, and bass playing in particular, were part of everyday conversation.

He told me the famous double bass joke about the bass player who goes to the opera to hear *Carmen*, and the next day his friends say to him, 'What was it like?' And he says, 'Oh, it is jolly good. You know when we get that tune going bom, bom, bom? There is another tune going on: dum, di di, dum, dum . . .'

After my grandmother died, grandfather wasn't looking after

himself, so I moved in and cooked proper meals for him, and we talked a lot. One day, when he was ninety, he didn't feel well. The doctor felt around his stomach and found a lump – it was cancer. There was no chance by them of operating or doing anything, and in two weeks he was dead.

I joined the LPO three years ago. My predecessor was a man called Bill Webster; he had been working with the LPO for twenty-five years as principal bass and suddenly had a heart attack and died. He was a great, big, strapping man, seemed in very good trim, and the last bloke you would expect to have a heart attack.

The LPO bass section is a reflection of Bill, who appointed most of them. There are six members and two associate members. Bryan, the number two, is an extremely nice man, very comfortable to sit next to. He is very soft-centred; he shies away from anything unpleasant, he will only watch a film or an opera if it has got a happy ending. A lot of music can be interesting, but dissonant: I don't think that would appeal much to Bryan, because he likes everything sugary-sweet.

Then, we have got Lawrie. He lives up in Blackheath with his wife who is a cellist. He is into Tai-Chi, and we call him the Jesus freak, as he has a big beard. I get on very well with him, he is a good laugh and keeps us very well entertained. When rehearsals or sessions are getting boring, he is a master of a thing where you put your finger on the G string, and bow between the nut and the finger so the note is extremely high. He can play almost any violin solo you like on his bass with astonishing accuracy.

David James is extremely quiet, quite nervous, a very nice man; and Geoff Downes is the great philosopher, so he has always got a point of view about everything. George, the number four, is a very nice man.

I don't think you will find anything out about Ken Goode, if you talked to him all day. I sat next to him for a year and didn't learn anything about him. I think he has lost sight of Ken himself.

He was number two, and he is now number six. There was a bass solo from Mahler's First Symphony, which he wouldn't play. He said he would rather pull his own head off than play that bass solo – and you couldn't have somebody sitting at number two who was refusing to do part of their job.

The LPO repertoire is heavily based on the German romantic tradition, which is great for the bass. We did *The Messiah* last year, which is marvellous to play, you always get a good bass line there.

When you listen to music, you don't think, 'Oh, I will listen to those basses', but we are underpinning everything. It is like a house, you don't see the foundations, but they are very important, and if you take them away, the structure falls to pieces.

We are doing Mahler 9 next week. I don't know it, so I went and bought a tape, and I have been painting the spare room listening to Mahler 9. It is a marvellous piece, and I've been thinking, oh yes, that will be good to play. Of course, that depends on the conductor, they dictate everything, how loud, how soft, how fast, how slow.

Hopefully, Tennstedt will be conducting. He has got a great mixture of brain and heart, he understands music, he performs with his soul, and there is always going to be a wonderful performance with him. He has had terrible ill health, and every time he conducts it is as though it might be the last time. He cancelled his last two performances. It may be that we will never see him again.

Josephine St Leon
Viola

'Shostakovich 5 is very Shostakovichy'

WHEN I WENT to music school I played the flute, but they had millions of flute players, so I thought I would try the viola. I stuck with it because I rather liked the sound it makes. I never really liked the flute, and I got bored with it: it seemed such a limited instrument, the dynamic range is very small. All my flute-playing friends will hate me for saying this.

My dad used to play the violin, he thought he was a marvellous musician, but he was terrible. He pushed me all the time. It wasn't good enough to practise half an hour a day, it had to be three hours a day, which I resented immensely. That's why I nearly did an Arts degree and became a journalist or something, but then I thought, well, it is a bit stupid not to do something you are good at, simply to go against your father.

When my parents split, I went to live with my mother. She certainly encouraged me, but she didn't force me – she let me get on with it myself. In fact, she was marvellous.

My viola teacher was the one who really motivated me to do all the practice. He wasn't a great technical teacher, but he made you play things because he wanted you to play them. He would hand me a concerto which was much too difficult and say, 'Go and learn this'. You would feel you had let him down badly if you couldn't play it by the time you came back. He got me

167

involved in all sorts of other things, too. He conducted a youth orchestra, which I played in, and he used to give me chamber music coaching for nothing. If he decided you were one of his favourites, which I was, then he did everything for you. I think it was the first time I got the impression I was important to someone.

Rite of Spring was the first thing I did with the LPO. At the time, I sat next to a lady who was deaf and played everything a semi-tone flat, but I am happy to say she left shortly after. This orchestra makes a wonderful sound, it is very exciting to be in the orchestra sometimes.

We violas are vital, of course! We don't get spectacular amounts of solos, but we provide all the harmony and all the interesting little bits that happen in the middle. In the Mozart operas, everybody is jealous of the violas, because we have these wonderful parts to play, with amazing harmony notes in the middle.

Most of the other sections don't appreciate violas. They all make viola jokes, like: what is the definition of a gentleman? . . . Somebody who can play the viola, but doesn't. This is all because years and years ago, viola players were failed violinists, but that is not true any more.

Viola players are dead swotty. I will never forget coming back from a tour – I had no part in this, I promise – and the viola section were huddled at the back of the plane, compiling a list of all the viola concertos they knew. As a rule, viola players tend not to drink very much, and they seriously worry about fingerings and bowings, and all the rest of it.

I sit in between Robert Duncan and Mimi Davis. Mimi is fairly serious as a rule but, fortunately, she is not when she's with me, so we sit and gossip. I have to be a bit more serious with Robert, because he keeps discussing music, and asking me what I think of the bowings.

If I don't like the music, I get pissed off. I am not keen on commercial work, light-music sessions and film sessions are dreadfully tedious – but they are very lucrative, so I just think about the bank balance.

If we have got a conductor who isn't very good, and does pieces I like badly, then I think to myself, what am I doing here? There are millions of conductors I don't like. A conductor can really spoil it for you, he can take everything at the wrong speed, or he can be too interfering. Being an orchestral musician is frustrating because you are always being told what to do by the conductor, or playing the way the principal wants.

But mostly I like the music we play. Haitink is magical, and Haitink doing Shostakovich 5 always sticks in my memory.

Shostakovich 5 is very Shostakovichy, it has got a horrible viola tune that is way up the top of the viola, and there are difficult shifts – which Robert Duncan practises endlessly, whether we are doing it or not. It is very bleak, but it is also very exciting, and I love the combination of Haitink and Shostakovich.

Haitink has got an extraordinary way with words. Some conductors can talk and talk and talk, and you sit there, and you're not much wiser at the end. Haitink says a few words, and you think, oh, so *that* is how I should be playing it. He'll say: 'It is like a heartbeat,' or 'It is dawn on a beach,' or, 'Imagine the cat got the canary' – it can be something arty-farty or incredibly stupid, but whatever it is, he just encapsulates it somehow.

Bryan Scott
Double Bass

'Never ask a musician to dance'

I LEFT SCHOOL at fourteen, to take up an apprenticeship in a piano firm in Walthamstow. I learned a lot about the different kinds of actions, the difference between the cheap pianos and the expensive ones.

There were some beautiful pianos in the shop, Bösendorfers, Steinways, Bechsteins, and there was a Blüthner I liked very much. I bought that – on the never-never of course – it cost about £200, which seemed an absolute fortune at the time.

Unfortunately I had to leave after about eighteen months, because I was ill with asthma. The primary job of an apprentice is to clean the pianos out – you can imagine how dirty they were – and the dust really upset me.

When I was nineteen, I got a scholarship to the Royal Academy of Music, playing the piano. The principal asked if I wanted a second instrument. I said, no, but he insisted: 'Oh, you must have a second instrument, you're a nice tall chap, we'll put you on the bass.' And that's how I came to play the bass.

I didn't take much interest in it at first, because I was mad keen on playing the piano, but gradually, I got more interested, and by the time I left school, I thought of myself as a bass player.

It's a lovely instrument, the bass, I enjoy playing it very much, I must say. It hasn't got the beauty of a cello. A cello can sing so wonderfully, and bring a tear to the eye, and touch your heart. I can't say the bass can do that, but it can get pretty near it, it has a very rich, wonderful sound, and as an orchestral instrument it adds such a bloom to the whole sound. Orchestras sound very thin without basses.

Most of the really great composers wrote very effectively for the bass. We've been playing some Wagner this morning, and he wrote wonderfully for the bass; Shostakovich has this wonderful, shifting, slow bass line, and there are quite a few well-known bass solos, like the Frère-Jacques tune in Mahler 1, Second Movement.

Work is the first thing you think about when you leave the Academy. I did nearly eighteen months freelancing, any job that came along.

I played at Scarborough one summer, which is where I met my Doris. She was managing a little café, selling ice creams, and she knew musicians were penniless, and used to give me free ice creams. After that summer, whenever I had a free day, I would drive from London to Scarborough, which was a six-hour journey in the days before motorways.

It was a very spartan thing, my Ford Popular. There was no heater, and the windscreen wipers worked on an airtank that was fed from the throttle, so that when you put your foot on the accelerator, the windscreen wipers stopped – just when you needed them most.

I'd feel pretty exhausted once I got there, but I would go to her parents' house and have something to eat, and they would make a fuss of me, and we'd then go out and have a dance. Mind you, never ask a musician to dance, because they're the worst dancers in the world, with the least sense of rhythm, which is strange, isn't it?

On one of my day trips, I took Doris out for a drive over the moors. I had bought a ring, and I asked her to close her eyes, and hold out her hand, and I put the ring on, and asked, 'Will you marry me?' We're still married, and I'm still in love.

★   ★   ★

I've been in the orchestra now for twenty-seven years. When I first joined the LPO, it was a very tightly knit orchestra, everybody was great pals. For instance, when we went on tour, if you felt like going out for a meal you would wait at the bottom of the lift in the hotel, and to the first person who came out of the lift, you'd say, 'Fancy a bite?' and they'd say 'Great', and off you would go. But now, most of the younger players, especially the violinists, tend to stick together in groups.

I'll be sixty on 14 May, and I'd like to play less. We work so hard at times, and I feel I shouldn't be flogging myself doing film sessions and recordings, which are very hard work, and unrewarding musically. I'd like to just do the concerts and, also, move back in the section. But I wouldn't stop though, because I love it so much. I'd like to be playing when I die.

Meanwhile, I have a great deal to enjoy at home. I have my lathe, and I make telescopes: I grind and polish the lenses, and all that is very interesting. I looked at Saturn the other night, and it was incredible, like a little jewel. I've looked at Jupiter and seen the red spot, and I nearly always look at the moon when it comes up – from my house I get a marvellous view of the moon rising up just over the church. All these things are wonderful to look at, and it produces a great sense of awe in me when I look into the night sky.

John Sharp
Cello

'Beethoven and Brahms are fine, but they are dead . . .'

MY FATHER WAS a fishmonger. He went off with another woman when I was less than a year old.

I learned to play the piano when I was five. I am not sure how keen I was, I am not sure how keen I am about music at all, I have got deep reservations about it as an art form.

I didn't really want music to be my career. I auditioned for RADA, and had been accepted, but my mother and stepfather had very forceful ways of making sure I didn't go: I was bullied, suffered physical and emotional blackmail, the whole works. My whole childhood, my whole youth really, was totally frustrated by either my mother or stepfather. I don't want to go too much into these things. Let's just say my stepfather was an extremely violent man. He once knocked out my two front teeth, so I am reminded of his violence every morning of my life as I put in the false ones.

I was eleven when my mother married my stepfather. The only reason they got married was because she was pregnant. I immediately had premonitions that was going to be a very bad time . . . I saw the quality of their relationship. And from the age of eleven to seventeen, I experienced all sorts of stuff, with the police and the NSPCC constantly called in.

I can see quite clearly now that my mother needed that sort of confrontational, quite violent relationship. It was part of her

175

own reality, and I would say that eventually people get what they need. They are still together, and they still have a very hot time. Well, if nothing else, it introduced me to the reality of the human condition, which tries to civilize itself with various social forms, like marriage and family.

Nowadays, I pick up my cello rather as I suppose a stone breaker picks up the mallet. Working in an orchestra is extremely hard work, absolutely back-breaking, but I have two children to support . . .

The need for the orchestra to earn money to pay its bills means we have to work all hours, night and day, all locations on the globe. Sometimes I leave for work at 8 o'clock in the morning and return home at 2 a.m. – and then quite often we are expected to be at the Festival Hall for rehearsal early the following morning.

This amount of work has dire consequences for relationships. You can't run a marriage along those lines; marriage is a very conventional thing, marriage needs a nine-to-five normality, which musicians cannot give to it.

I managed to sustain my marriage for twelve years, which was quite amazing, and by today's standards is quite a reasonable amount of time. But there is no way I would fit a marriage or any sort of relationship or commitment into my life now, I realize that you can't share our sort of life with anybody – it is no life.

It takes a good conductor to move me. Tennstedt, in all my experience of orchestral playing, is the only conductor to have managed to step outside his own silly little ego. Most of them are egomaniacs, like Solti, who I think is poison.

Tennstedt has his flaws, and his major flaw, of course, is that he is German, which means that he is a hypochondriac, because all Germans are hypochondriacs. Maybe he has been ill, but he indulges himself too much, so he is rarely in London these days to conduct us. But then he says, 'Okay, Mahler 7 . . .' and it only takes this man to lift his hands and the orchestra produces

for him a sound that it produces for no one else. I can't explain
how or why it happens, the atmosphere in the hall, the audience
satisfied, Tennstedt absolutely worn out, you just know somehow this is what Mahler would have wanted. For me, Klaus
Tennstedt is just the greatest thing there ever was.

I do have serious doubts about being in a museum all the time.
I mean Beethoven and Brahms are fine, but they are dead, I am
alive. I want music to interact with social reality. I want people
to write things like 'A Song Cycle of the Dustman', I mean that
seriously. Any decent art form has to interact with reality, and
by permanently going back to the museum, we are not doing
that.

Music is at least two hundred years out of date and behind the
times, we are still in the time of Mozart. Okay, let's play the
museum, but let's have a percentage of our time put towards
building new edifices.

Art discovered 150 years ago that art is what the artist says is
art, not what the dilettante and the people who hold the purse
strings think. Music hasn't discovered that yet. And until music
can get out there in the marketplace and interact with social and
intellectual reality, as people like Monet did in the art world,
then it is dead. In order for music to live, it has got to come
alive in the hearts and mind and souls of the musicians.

Julian Shaw
Viola

'Not to take anything away from Steve . . .'

BY THE TIME I went to the Royal College of Music, I was very large, my hands were huge, and I was having trouble with the violin. I knew I was never going to be a virtuoso violinist, and when my professor suggested I try the viola, it was a wonderfully liberating experience, because it was much more my size. I became very attracted to its sound qualities, and suddenly realized that this was my instrument.

Basically, it is just like a big violin. It is physically more demanding because of its size, it requires more weight in the bow arm, and a different kind of bow attack, but it opened up a lot of possibilities which were not available to me as a violinist. For instance, it is tricky to do very fast passage work on the violin if you have got large hands, because the notes are very close together at the top of the instrument, whereas a viola has got a longer string length, so there's more room to move your fingers around. I made a very rapid technical improvement.

For years and years I was looking for a viola, and one day I went along to a Sotheby's sale. There was a big room with trestle tables heaped with piles of violin and viola cases with lot numbers on them. I looked at one particular instrument which was dusty and dirty, and had only one string. From past experience I had taken along some extra strings, and although there were a lot of people in the room, I played a bit, and I knew instantly it was fantastic. I bid for it the following week and I've had it ever since. It was made in Cremona, northern Italy, where Stradivari and Guarneri worked. It is just an exceptional instrument; it gives me immense pleasure to play. It is like being given the best paintbrush and the best paints, so you can create all sorts of colours which you hadn't even thought of before.

I am number four viola. I had applied for the number three job, but Steve Broom got it. He came from outside. As it happens we get on very well, but I certainly was not consulted about it. I had been in the orchestra eleven years, and you get typecast, it becomes almost impossible to get promotion within your own section. So I have to make a choice as to whether I am going to stay in the orchestra, or move out and then come back in again at a higher position. Steve has done very well by job-hopping.

That is all past history now. At the time, it was deeply hurtful, of course, it always is when you are overlooked. But I just can't be bothered with that any more. Besides, I have already been a principal in Scotland, I have recorded, I have done all sorts of things.

By coincidence Steve Broom and I were both in the finals for a job at Covent Garden. He has got down to the final few now, although he still doesn't know yet whether he will get the job. But it has cost him a fortune financially. We only get paid for the work we do, so he would have to take up a block of work to do an audition, and now he is faced with a trial, which is going to lose him even more.

Of course, I was disappointed, I am sure I could have done it as well as anybody else. But it is not as simple as that. Not to take any credit away from Steve, I didn't know anybody at the Garden, I don't know any of the people on the jury. And, again, not taking anything away from Steve, but Steve is very good friends with the principal.

For me an orchestra is somewhere I earn my money. Personally, I would prefer to play chamber music.

Essentially, I love music more than I love the orchestra. Ninety per cent of concerts are what I call craftsmanship concerts, you do them as well as you can, and it is unlikely the earth is going to move. The time the earth moves for me is when I am playing violin duets at seven o'clock in the morning with my eight-year-old daughter, or when I am playing a concerto with a not very good semi-professional orchestra who are in love with music. We had a marvellous chamber-music evening at home last night, which went on until well after midnight.

Hopefully, in another few years I should have made enough money not to have to go into the orchestra and be bogged down by the petty politics and trivia. I would miss the great performances though, and the great conductors.

If you put a bad conductor in front of us, the orchestra will put their heads down and produce a standard performance. Most of us know the repertoire backwards anyway – if you put an egg-beater in front of us, we would produce a good performance.

But Klaus Tennstedt is someone who opened up a completely new vista for me. He is so ill that he can't conduct any more – but he never relied on conducting. A great conductor is not someone who stands and beats four in a bar. A great conductor has an enormous creative vision, and you become a channel for that through him.

What he does with Mahler is life itself, it is a huge journey where you experience a total world. Take Mahler 8, which we have just performed. It is such a huge score. Klaus, a man who has been ill for the last ten years, dodders out on to the stage, brings the baton down, and you see ahead of you this enormous span of life. And you come to the end of Mahler 8, and there is nothing else, that is it, the end. Those sort of experiences are phenomenal, and he is the only one that can do it.

Owen Slade

Tuba

'Mine was thirty-eight inches deflated and forty-four inches inflated. She said she had never seen anything like it'

IN MY FIRST YEAR at school I played the violin for a couple of weeks. I then had a fight with my brother, and hit him with it, and broke it, and they gave me a tuba after that.

It was like a duck to water straightaway. I took it home and started playing it, and I overheard my mum saying to my dad, 'What are we going to do about this?' It *was* a racket. But I practised every day at school and the next weekend I took it home again, and I remember Mum saying, 'Oh, that sounds a lot better.'

My mum and dad were fantastic, they supported me through the whole lot. Because I couldn't get it on the bus, they used to drive me anywhere, any time.

It took over my life, all I wanted to do was play the tuba. I was playing virtually every night of the week with different bands and orchestras, and during every break at school I used to practise.

I really liked the sound of it. When you play a short note, 'bomp', it's like an apple dropping into a bowl of cold custard, which is a very beautiful sound, actually. And in the high register, there's a singing baritone quality which is gorgeous.

Breath control and quantity of breath is what you need to play the tuba; you've got to be able to get enough breath down it. It's about five times longer than the trumpet, so you need five times more air.

I went to the doctor to have a medical for our mortgage, and she wanted to measure my ribcage, deflated and inflated. Mine was thirty-eight inches deflated and forty-four inches inflated. She said she'd never seen anything like it – I think she was a bit shocked.

In the orchestra, the tuba is generally used as background, it's the bass of the brass section, and also gives the double basses a kick up the backside.

Prokofiev seemed to know what he was doing when he was writing for the tuba. The tuba part in *Alexander Nevsky* is loud and low – you feel as if you're actually contributing something – Prokofiev's Fifth Symphony has a brilliant tuba part. Bruckner and Mahler use the tuba to its full capacity, they understood what it could do.

I love working in studios. The last thing we were doing was *Cliffhanger*, a film by Sylvester Stallone. If you watched a film without music, it would be boring, you need us there to build up the tension in all the different scenes. In *Cliffhanger*, there was someone falling off a cliff, several planes exploding, people hanging on cliffs, someone got cut with a knife and shot, a couple of people were harpooned. There were some good tunes in it as well, the theme tune was fantastic.

I'd highly recommend you see that film . . . and you can hear the LPO too, no extra charge.

Stephen Smith

Guitar

'Her husband found out eventually . . .'

I WAS AT SCHOOL in Liverpool. The Beatles' legacy was still strong and, like most people, I picked up the guitar and played in school bands. I was more drawn to heavier rock, bands like Yes and Led Zeppelin, and taught myself to read music from song books and worked out with the records. I most liked a fairly unfashionable band called Wishbone Ash who played West Coast-influenced music mixed with English folk as well. They wrote more extended pieces, which were structurally challenging, more musically based.

There was no particular musical interest in my family. Dad was in management at Wall's, he was involved in the production of sausages and pork pies primarily . . . which might have something to do with my being a vegetarian, come to think of it.

For my fourteenth birthday I was given a very old Horner acoustic guitar, which was a great disappointment, because I was hoping for an electric guitar. But two years later, I had saved enough to buy an electric guitar from Frank Hessey's in Liverpool, it was a Squire Stratocaster copy – and fairly rough and ready. It was very difficult to keep in tune and had a very difficult playing action.

It took a little while to get an amplifier sorted out, so I used to play it through the hi-fi, which is not really recommended – the speakers were blown to pieces, I'm afraid.

I think I plumped for the Stratocaster because they were offering three free guitar lessons with a purchase. And those three lessons went on to develop into a longer course of study with that particular teacher. He was a great teacher, and a fine musician, I don't really know why he was teaching in an electric guitar shop.

When the careers' teacher asked what I wanted to do, I said, 'play the guitar', and he made some inquiries about taking it beyond an initial interest. He came up with a place which ran O- and A-level-based music courses, and that was great. The principal there was a very strong influence musically, and she made me listen to classical music, Brahms and Beethoven.

My dad would drop me off at my course before going into work. On the way up, we would have big rows about music. He used to talk about Gene Kruper, who was a drummer in the big bands, as being the best, and I would counter with Ian Pace, the drummer from Deep Purple, who I felt was technically far superior because he could play louder, and for longer.

At school I decided to concentrate totally on work, which seemed to be necessary to get up to the standard of certain other guitar players in my form. For two years, I just shut myself away, I was very self-motivated.

I didn't go out with a single woman during that period, I was completely celibate. It was a kind of Samson thing, really: I had to completely devote myself to music, and if I was distracted by any other activity, I would be less pure. It was kind of romantic, and attractive, and it was a challenge too.

I started writing music as well at that point. A lot of the stuff seemed to be very solitary. I wrote pieces inspired by night, by darker aspects of life. The guitar is a strange instrument, it is capable of being very intimate, and yet very big as well, it can entertain vast crowds of people in a stadium, and yet draw people in.

In the end, I was successful beyond my wildest dreams – I was accepted by the Royal Northern College of Music in Manchester. Once there, it was a baptism of fire. I had thought I must be pretty good, because I had got into this prestigious college. But

I could see that I was just a small fish, that this was only the beginning, and I had a long, long way to go.

I did fairly well for two years, I still had the same head-down attitude. But then I reached a sort of burn out by the end of the second year and, in the third year, I started taking in a few of the things I'd been missing out on in my school years, like women and parties . . . basically, letting my hair down.

I got involved with a married woman, which was very complicated. At the time I was twenty, and she was twenty-five, which seemed a big difference.

It was a complete extreme: from having no experience of women to going out with an older, married woman. It wasn't a very easy period in my life, but it was exciting.

The husband found out eventually, of course, and made all sorts of threats.

In the end, I just scraped through college; that relationship just zapped my energy away from music. The problem was I couldn't keep it in context, not having any experience on how to deal with an affair of that nature.

My married lady and I parted company more or less straight after I moved to London, and I am involved with someone now, although I still retain my independence. I hope eventually to raise a family, I keep thinking time is going on, although I'm only thirty-three.

Joakim Svenheden

Leader

'We once skated from Uppsala to Stockholm'

I WAS BORN in the south of Sweden, then moved up to Söderhamn. My father was a surgeon, he played the piano a little bit, although he wasn't very good.

We had a rock 'n' roll group, me and my brother. Non-Toxic we called ourselves – we saw it on a pen, and thought, yeah, that's it. I played electric bass, he played the guitar, and there was a drummer, a singer and an organist as well. We wrote one or two blues melodies ourselves, but mostly we did cover versions, things like Deep Purple, Led Zeppelin and Judas Priest. It was a lot of fun.

First, I was with the Stockholm Chamber Orchestra, a very good group, and we went on tour all over the world. And then I was leading the Norrköping Symphony Orchestra; that's where I met the musical director of this orchestra, who invited me over.

Now after six months at the LPO, I start to feel a little bit at home. But I miss hearing the Swedish language. Perhaps if you move to a country at my age, you never feel at home in a new place. I'm thirty-two this summer, so I'm not old, but I'm not young.

My mother and father visited me a couple of weeks ago, and my brother just left two days ago. He's an engineer now, so he's into other things, but he plays the guitar still, and we went to a shop called Vintage Guitar and spent the whole afternoon trying out old electric guitars. It was like the good old days.

It's difficult to forget your roots. My family have a summer house just south of Göteborg, on the Kattegat, and it's very nice, it has the most beautiful scenery.

I miss windsurfing there, and I miss most of all the winter when we go skating on the lakes, with the long skates. Do you know this sport? It's fantastic. You can skate on ice for miles and miles and miles. You check where the wind is blowing, and then with the wind at your back, you can go from town to town. We once skated from Uppsala to Stockholm.

Swedish girls are very different from English women. In Swedish girls you can see something in their eyes – nature maybe, the trees and the forests, a mirror of what you've been growing up in.

There's only one girl in the orchestra who has that look . . .

Angela Tennick
Oboe

'Being a clergyman's daughter . . .'

I GOT MARRIED TOO EARLY, I was very silly. I had these ideas of marriage being wonderful and comfortable, and I was perhaps the last generation where if you weren't engaged to be married by the age of twenty-one, you were 'on the shelf'. I really did worry about that. I felt, I have got to find somebody, because I hadn't a lot of confidence on my own.

I think that partly goes back to when I was a child. I had a very clever older brother who went to Oxford, while I failed the eleven-plus.

I had regrets even before I married him, but being a clergyman's daughter, I couldn't go back on it. I should have done. I was far too naïve to be taking those sort of vows, I hadn't experienced anything of life whatsoever. I just wish my parents had stopped me.

Things very soon started to go wrong. We argued all the time, and neither of us had any experience of sex, so that side of things was a disaster as well.

Another reason why it didn't work was because I realized he would never make it as a professional musician. I have to respect who I am with, as a person *and* as a musician. We worked together in a wind quintet, and I used to get absolutely frustrated by his awful sense of rhythm.

Jonathan came along, but things didn't get any better, and I

191

had very bad depression after he was born, which didn't help.

I began doing the odd bit of chamber music, and my husband decided to start a music shop. I was not very happy about that, he was running it with a woman, and after a while, I thought something was going on there. But I just couldn't believe he would do anything. I had been brought up in an honest, church environment: when you are married, you don't do things like that.

When I found letters, it hit me very hard. But as soon as I had proof, I said, right, I want a divorce.

The break was made and it was absolutely awful, dreadful.

I always say it was a miracle, because just at this really difficult time, I was asked to come into the LPO. I remember getting a message on my answering machine: 'Would I come and do a date in Eastbourne?'

I was terrified. I hated the idea of orchestras, I was nervous of conductors, and big audiences . . . I told them I was busy!

But they asked me again, and the first date I did with the LPO was *Rite of Spring*, playing third oboe. That was in the Festival Hall, and I don't know how I kept my nerve!

After that I started to go in more and more regularly. 'Would I like to do some Glyndebourne?' And I did two operas, and that was very nice, because I got to know people in the orchestra.

Then it was suggested I might like to do a huge, all-around-Europe tour, and I went along, and had the most wonderful time.

Also, I met somebody, and that was a real high, it was wonderful. I had an affair, which was two weeks of absolute bliss – at my lowest ebb, it gave me such self-confidence. It couldn't have worked though, he was married.

After the tour I was appointed full time, and life just went, *whoosh*. I loved the orchestra, and the social side of it, and touring.

And I met Robert, who plays in the viola section, and we hit it off straightaway. I had always liked him when I talked to him, he seemed such a nice chap, and we had the same sense of humour. But although I liked him, I wasn't sure whether he was the right person for me. Also, I had to get some things out of my system first. But, eventually, having been let down by one or two people, I suddenly thought: what am I doing? Robert is fond of me, and I like him, and then it all sort of developed.

We tried to keep it quiet to begin with but, of course, as soon as there's any sort of gossip like that, it's round very quickly.

I can remember in America, when we had only just started to go out, we got the rehearsal time wrong, and walked in together late. Of course, everyone made the most of it, shuffling and making suggestive noises, the string section knocking their bows against the strings.

We have a very good relationship. Most couples quite like to get away from their partners from time to time, but Robert and I, we are together just about all the time.

Sometimes I wish I wasn't a second oboe: there aren't many solos to play. But, at the same time, I don't think I could cope with the stress. I have had enough stress in my life, I don't want any more.

You can play well or badly depending on whether you have a good or bad reed, and I spend my life making reeds. Each cane, being a living thing, is different. You might get a reed which seems lovely, but when you play, suddenly, it makes a hissing sort of noise, and the conductor says, 'Frying tonight!'

When I do have a solo, I imagine I am sitting at home playing to myself, and no one else is there. It is just one of the techniques I have of trying to combat my nerves, because if I suddenly thought, God, there are two or three thousand people in this hall, I have a conductor and an orchestra waiting for me to make a mistake . . . I couldn't play a note.

Stephen Trier
Clarinet

'Huge, great steaks, and all kinds of fresh fruit . . .'

IN 1950, I WAS STARTING my fourth year at the Royal College of Music when I had the most extraordinary stroke of luck. Sir Thomas Beecham was setting off with his orchestra, the Royal Philharmonic, to do an enormous tour of the USA, and they couldn't find anybody to play a bass clarinet. I was invited to join them – I wasn't even asked to do an audition, I just went along and played some concerts, and that was that. It was a very eminent woodwind section in those days, and I can remember being absolutely terrified. But it was a very good start, I was extraordinarily fortunate.

Thomas Beecham was an amazing musician, an amazing conductor, there is nobody like him around today, and probably never will be.

He was a diminutive man, when he sat on a stool, his legs didn't touch the ground. He had a full head of hair, a beard, and an amazing twinkle in his eyes.

He had this extraordinary gift of actually making you play better than you knew how to, it was true charlatanism – a charlatan being somebody who produces something out of nothing – and he did it with enormous charm. An awful lot of the other conductors I have worked for have been terrible bullies, but he was incredibly patient. I remember him saying in rehearsal when something wasn't going quite right, 'I can't seem to follow you . . .' That was all there was to it: with him, a nod was as good as a wink.

In a sense, he is responsible for the orchestral play-offs that exist in London now. Every single orchestra in London, with the exception of the BBC Symphony, was a creation of, or saved by Beecham. In the 1920s, he salvaged the LSO. They then wanted their own independence, so he started the LPO, and after the war he came back and founded two more, with the Philharmonia as a vehicle to make records. He saw off two or three fortunes of his own, and quite a number of other people's as well.

Well, it is hard to think back to being a twenty-year-old after all these years, but to find myself in an orchestra which was a stunning band, and playing in places like Carnegie Hall, was amazing. We went over on the *Queen Mary*, which was a style of life one had never experienced before. We came from a drab, post-war London, where a lot of people still had their black-out shutters because they hadn't got the money to pay for cloth to make decent curtains. It was amazing to see the lavishness of the food in America – huge, great steaks, and all kinds of fresh fruit – while Britain went on being rationed long after other countries we had beaten in the war were doing very nicely.

I had been given introductions to people in America and they were extraordinarily kind and friendly, I was quite overwhelmed. One night, we were doing a concert and some guys came over to me at the end and shouted, 'Come back and stay the night,' and I stayed in their fraternity house at Cornell, where they were having a barn dance.

It was a thirteen-week tour, we performed six concerts a week, and Beecham, then in his mid-seventies, conducted every one of them. Can you imagine any of these highly pampered conductors doing that today? They make so much money anyway they don't need to. I don't suppose Beecham ever made any money out of that trip, I don't imagine he took a fee.

Most important of all, one was elated by the concerts. Audiences in those days were all wildly enthusiastic, they were much less blasé than they are now. Nowadays, the audience is rather like the jaded girl who says, 'Go on, thrill me . . .'

At sixty-three, I am one of the oldest in the orchestra, the players have become very young. In American or Continental orchestras you see quite a lot of older players, but I think here the actual stress and strain of being a musician kills off a lot of us old-timers.

As for the music, it is just not such fun as it used to be. It isn't exciting performing Beethoven's Ninth Symphony any more, for instance. In 1950, Beethoven's Ninth was an enormous event, whereas now it is probably being played every two minutes somewhere in the world. At this very moment there are probably fifteen orchestras whizzing on an aeroplane from one place in the world to another.

Also, there is an enormous amount of music going on, everybody's got rows and rows of CDs they can turn on at the flick of a finger – there aren't enough hours in the day to play the amount of recordings most people possess. I just wonder whether you perhaps debase the currency by using too much of it.

I often ask myself if it is getting time for me to move out. I sometimes feel that this *is* a young man's game. I look with a certain amount of horror at trips to South Africa and long tours like that, and I would prefer to stay put. I really am beginning to feel that I have been at it too long, but what else one does instead, I don't know.

I used to have a workshop at the bottom of my garden in which I did quite a lot of work, wood-turning and things like that. But I've lost a bit of heart over that because a friend, who was forever helping me, died last year, and it has been rather traumatic knowing I can't ring him up to get me out of trouble.

The aspect of music that I do still enjoy enormously is the teaching. We have got some astonishingly good students, and I must say that my wife and I derive enormous pleasure from my ex-students, quite a number of whom have become great pals.

The passion of my life is our place in France, which is about an hour south of Amboise. It's a cowshed really, but it has lovely trees, a fairly large garden and, generally speaking, it is a wonderful spot. The French may not necessarily be your favourite race, but my goodness, they have so many things that one covets.

I am rather depressed at the moment, because I feel anxious about the music business. I am not over-brimming with confidence about orchestras in general. The symphony orchestra has to be supported by enormous funds, I don't know anybody who thinks that an orchestra could possibly make a profit, and I think it increasingly unlikely that people will continue to put money into orchestras.

Music has got so many parasites attached to it now, and filling the hall costs so much, that hardly a single concert makes money – mainly because the conductors are all paid far too much, much more than they are worth.

Bob Truman
Principal Cello

'Energy crisis, Bob . . .'

MY PARENTS WERE very average, loving, easy-going Austra-
lians. My father drove a fork-lift truck at Woolworth's; I am
very proud to tell you that, because people who get to the top
jobs are usually from a musical background. The fact that I have
become principal cello of the London Philharmonic is nothing
short of a miracle.

My school was as rough as they come, rough as bags. I loved
painting, I was an instinctive, creative sort of person, and there
was no scope for children like that in the early 1960s in Australia.
But when I was thirteen, we got a fantastic music teacher, he
was like a diamond in a dung heap, and he got me singing in
Gilbert and Sullivan operas, which I loved. And he said, 'You
have got a marvellous ear, I want you to study an instrument,
because you could have a career.'

There was only a cello left, and my hands were a bit
small, but within two lessons I liked it, and he pushed me to
a very old, retired cellist who gave me lessons on the weekends.

I hated school so much I finished at fifteen, and then my life
just fell into a great big abyss. I had to earn my living, and I
took a job where I had to wrap parcels all day – it was a dog's
life. I then took a job in a violin-making business. I served cus-
tomers, sold violins, bows, rosin and strings, I swept the floor

and cleaned up at night, and I practised every morning between five and eight at home.

At sixteen, something quite wonderful happened. After work I used to wash up in my auntie's restaurant, and her lover was a married man whose daughter was married to the top male cellist in Australia. And he said to me, 'The cello is a virtuoso instrument, you either have to do it properly or not at all.' And I started formal cello lessons when I was seventeen, and the whole world opened up to me.

I began playing freelance with the Sydney Symphony Orchestra. The early 1970s was the beginning of the big film industry in Australia, there were twenty-two film companies, and we were very busy playing film scores.

Meanwhile, things were very, very difficult in our family. My father had bowel cancer, my sister got pregnant – announced at seventeen she was going to have a baby – everything hit us. Can you imagine? Your seventeen-year-old sister comes home and announces she is pregnant, while dad is in the front room dying of cancer.

After dad died, I came to London.

I flew over – Qantas of course, and was met by a friend and slept on the floor at his place. I didn't know what had hit me, I had never seen English grot. It was a bedsit in a horrible house, and I found the country terribly cold and grey. But I was devouring London. I saw everything. I was going to the theatre and the galleries, seeing all the legends of the concert platform who never went to Australia. I just loved it . . . England was my university.

I became a member of the London Symphony, I was on the back desk, the bald head in the flowers, and I ended up sitting on the platform with Emil Gill, and Rostropovich. They were very exciting days, André Previn came, and we were touring everywhere.

But I didn't fit into the LSO. They are very macho, a lot of drinking goes on, there was a whole lot of butching it up with the boys, and I just didn't feel happy there.

When I heard they wanted a principal cello in the London Philharmonic, I went for it.

My sadness as a concert cellist is that I spend a lot of my life playing music I don't like. Franz Welser-Möst is just crazy about Bruckner, I hate Bruckner. It bores me turgid. Great big Gothic turds. I said to Franz, 'I hope you are not going to end up hating me because I hate Bruckner,' and he said, 'Oh, it might come to that.'

I love the music that attracted me into the profession in the first place: Beethoven, Brahms, Ravel. Debussy is unconditionally great classical music. That is music for my soul, it is worthwhile. We do all this Mahler. Awful. Some of the Strauss tone poems, and *Ein Heldenleben* which we did recently, I loathe them, they ruin your bow arm, they ruin your intonation, you come off absolutely exhausted – Franz goes back to the Savoy with £6000 in his bag, and I feel fucked.

The conductor is absolutely everything. Solti makes you feel like shit: 'I am used to better in Chicago.' It doesn't matter what you give Solti, it is not good enough. Other people are unpleasant too.

I adore Tennstedt. Tennstedt is the daddy of the lot, the king, you just bleed for him, you'd bleed to death.

The thing I love Tennstedt for is the way he makes audiences sit up and listen to the classics, like Beethoven 5 or Beethoven's 'Eroica' symphony. These are standard repertoire pieces that he interprets as though he wrote them. He gets on the box, taps the rostrum, and he says, 'I will not have a repertoire performance, I will not.' Other conductors have become famous, like Previn, who did wonderful Rachmaninov and Walton, but he was never famous for his Brahms or Beethoven, the real classics. And that is why I will always love Tennstedt, because he took on the hardest repertoire and made it sound sparkling. His Mahler 5 live is sensational. Full of mistakes from beginning to end, people get tired, there are accidents, but, oh boy, that is a performance for all time.

Thank God, I played well last night. All principals feel insecure because there is such a thin line that divides excellence and catastrophe. It is a nerve-racking profession, it is an unforgiving profession. It doesn't matter how good you are as an orchestral leader, if you don't play your solos well, you are out, it is as simple as that. I have seen good people come and go because their playing went off . . . and you are only as good as your next performance.

I have recurring nightmares all the time: I can't get on to the concert platform, I can't find the steps. Another one is someone, usually the orchestral manager, slamming me up the stairs to play a concerto, and me saying, 'I can't remember the first fucking part . . .'

I live alone, I like living alone, but this career didn't help with meeting people. Most people who are alone tend to remain alone in our orchestra, and most single women seem to remain single. Hopeless hours, Glyndebourne, then we have tours on top of that. But, I always say, I live alone but I am not lonely. I have got my phone and, of course, the orchestra is a kind of family, there are people I am very fond of.

Santiago I adore. We are always in a car, lost in London, screaming and laughing. I have the world's worst sense of direction, it once took us six hours to get to Glyndebourne, we got completely lost. He was no help, of course.

John Sharp is absolutely fabulous. And he is the only cellist in London who can tap dance as well.

We are a pretty close bunch, except on tour. The orchestra is a different entity when it is touring. Crotchety. The stress factor is terrible, people become quite cranky. You drive four or five hours to the next town, starving, to find the restaurant is not open, and none of the beds are ready. You have a seating rehearsal at six, come back to find no restaurants are open until eight. So you do your concert, come back – to find the hotel restaurant closed at ten. So you take to the streets to find a restaurant, probably have a bit too much to drink, because you've been stressed. Go to bed well past midnight, and you are back on the coach at eight. Once you start doing that a couple of weeks at a time, you feel just awful.

The cello and music is the centre of my whole life. It has given me a lot – all the travel I have done, it is amazing. I have been to America alone fourteen times, I have been to Japan three or four times, I have been to China.

All in all, I am happy. I hate the climate from October to April, I get depressed, I have all the lights on in the winter. People say, 'Energy crisis, Bob!' I don't care, I'm Australian, I like light.

Franz Welser-Möst

Conductor

'I've a biography on Benjamin Britten, an encyclopaedia about holography, fairy tales by Selma Lagerlof, and an American book about Zen Buddhism . . .'

I HAVE TWO BROTHERS and two sisters, and we each learned an instrument. We lived in Linz, in Austria, which is an industrial town between Salzburg and Vienna.

I was a rather brainy child, and when I turned fourteen, my parents put me in a special music school, and I took up the violin, and after a few weeks, I knew that was what I wanted to do in my life.

The school orchestra was led by a man with enormous charisma; his teaching was not just restricted to the lessons, he was there for us twenty-four hours a day.

For some reason, he had the impression I might have a talent for conducting and, one day, he made me stand in front of my colleagues and conduct a Mozart Divertimento – Köchel-Verzeichnis 136, I remember it was. 'The earlier you learn these pieces,' he would say, 'the longer you live with them.'

When I was eighteen, I had a car accident and, after that, I couldn't play the violin properly any more.

I always call it my musical accident, because it happened on 19 November, and that was the date Schubert died, exactly one hundred and fifty years before.

It was a Sunday. A group of us had played a service in the morning, a Schubert Mass, and in the evening we were supposed to play the 'Trout' Quintet in a little town called Steyr, which was where Schubert had actually written it.

My best friend was driving. It was a bright but very chilly day, and the roads were very icy; suddenly, the car started to skid, and we went off the road, spinning round and around. It was quite a serious accident. My friend's mother died in it, she had been sitting next to me in the back. There were two girls in the car as well who broke all sorts of things, and my friend's father was there too, and he never recovered from that accident.

When we left the road, I hit the window and lost consciousness, thank God. Mother Nature's very good to us in such situations, all the thinking gets switched off, and you become like an animal, in the sense that you just fight for your life.

I woke up in the ambulance, and I remember my first thought was, 'Hopefully, we are going to make it to the concert . . .'

My friend, who was also quite badly hurt, was in the same ambulance as me. At one point he woke up and said, 'What has happened, was anyone hurt?' He didn't know . . .

I was put into intensive care, and they didn't know if I would survive, nor if I would be able to walk again, because I had no feelings in my legs.

That hospital in Steyr was a dreadful place. Two doctors began arguing, in front of me, as to what they should do with me. When I was eventually let out of intensive care, a nurse came in and ordered me to sit up for washing. I told her, 'Sorry, that's impossible . . .' whereupon she just yanked me up, and I heard a rasping noise from my back, and felt immense pain.

I called my father immediately, and said, 'Please, you've got to get me out of here . . .'

I was taken to another hospital, where they put me into plaster for twelve weeks, and I went back to school with my whole upper body in plaster, I looked like Hermann Munster.

I could sort of play the violin still, but two fingers on my left hand had become a bit sleepy, and would not work as fast as the others. I could play tunes, but technically difficult passages – no way. And so, eventually, I thought, 'Okay, I'll try something else,' and I went for conducting.

For me conducting was a natural gift. There's only a small amount of technique which can be learned, conducting is mostly about psychology, how you lead people, how you deal with people.

I learned from my teacher how to actually study a score. He told me to analyse the architecture and the harmonies, but never forget that everything you analyse at an intellectual level has to be translated to an emotional level, because that's the only level the audience will relate to when they go to a performance. They want to have an emotional experience.

I feel very emotional when I am conducting, sometimes I even cry on stage. What moves me the most is music from my home country, there's something about Schubert's Austrian melancholy which I enjoy.

I give the musicians a lot of freedom, which very often they think is a weakness on my part. It's actually the hardest option. It is much easier for a conductor to come in and say: 'I want this, this and this', end of story. But that's not great music-making. Many orchestral musicians get nervous if they're not told exactly what to do, but I think if you want to get to the creative forces inside the musician, you must give them a lot of freedom. Great music-making has to do with freedom and initiative, and everyone should be able to respond to the music and be galvanized on their own. They must all learn to take on that responsibility.

They will discover for themselves what I mean. It is a slow and difficult process, but when they have understood this truth, they will be better musicians.

★   ★   ★

Eight years ago, the LPO called and asked if I could step in for a conductor who had cancelled at very short notice.

Before I met them I was scared to death, I am always very nervous when I have to meet an orchestra for the first time, and I spent most of that night on the toilet.

It was the first top orchestra I had conducted, and it was incredible to hear that sort of sound. Compared to provincial orchestras, it was much more beautiful, much richer, there were more guts when they played.

In the first rehearsal, there was an incident with the principal flautist. Musicians always like to try out new conductors.

The flautist raised his arm. 'Yes please?' I said. He seemed to be talking to me, but I could hear no sound coming out, because there were people talking, it was very noisy. I said, 'Sorry, I can't hear you.' Suddenly, everyone went quiet, so it was dead silent, and he did exactly the same, just moving his lips, with no sound coming out. 'Oh, you mean I don't speak loud enough,' I said to him, and everyone laughed. To people who don't know about orchestral life, it seems like nothing, but in the confrontation between an orchestra and a conductor, there are many ways things can go. A lot of conductors would have lost their nerves in such a moment, or become angry . . . I just took it very calmly, and I had the guts to laugh at the joke. So I passed the test.

I do remember, when I flew back after that concert, I had the thought for the first time: now you're a real conductor.

I was invited back almost immediately. They asked if I would cover for a tour with Klaus Tennstedt, because by that time Klaus was ill and cancelling quite a lot. So I did that tour, and more and more concerts, until they asked if I would become music director.

Some of the musicians I know quite well, some of them I still have to do my homework and get to know better. One of my weakest points is a bad memory for names, I know 90 per cent of their names, but it still can happen that I go blank.

Unfortunately, life is so busy and hectic that you hardly ever get the chance after rehearsal to sit down, or have a drink, everyone just rushes off, and the only time I have a chance to talk to players is on tour.

We're going on a tour of Germany next week, actually, which I'm looking forward to. The great thing about tours is you always do the same programme, so you don't have to prepare that much for it, so there is more leisure time to talk and to read.

I've got a biography on Benjamin Britten to take with me, a book about holography which I've been wanting to read, fairy tales by Selma Lagerlof – who won the Nobel Prize in 1903 – and an American book about Zen Buddhism. It's a weird range, but I enjoy that.

Our last tour was to Japan. We had a magical moment in Tokyo. It was Beethoven 5, another occasion I had to step in at very short notice for Klaus – we only had one hour for rehearsal.

When I walked on stage for the performance, I was very on edge. I took my bow, turned around – and started right away, which was deliberately designed to take the orchestra by surprise. That meant there was no way for them to be careful, after all Beethoven 5 is a very risky piece, and you must do it that way, or it doesn't work.

It was a moment where the orchestra and I had to risk everything, it was like a car in a race taking every curve on two wheels – and we did it, it was one of the most fascinating performances, and I know a lot of the orchestra members think that also.

In fact, it was so exciting that the audience were yelling and screaming, which normally doesn't happen in Japan, and I became the first young conductor to have a big success there, because normally they only honour the old conductors.

The entire orchestra applauded me too because it had worked, and when I went off stage, a lot of players came up to me and said, 'congratulations, maestro,' and that was the first time they called me maestro.

★   ★   ★

Last season, there were quite a few mediocre performances, simply because I was not on form in many ways. I had bad health as a result of enormous psychological pressure: problems we had with our former managing director and his mistress, the former marketing director, plus, when it came to my artistic aims and thoughts, most of my ideas were just ignored by the management. And if you have no support for three years, it makes life almost impossible, and all my problems off stage started to come on stage.

Also, the press were very nasty about me. As always, when there's someone new and young, at first the British press say, 'he's great'. Then immediately after you begin to establish yourself, they try to knock you down.

If you look at reviews I get in the States, where they say, 'He's the maestro of the twenty-first century,' or, 'We haven't seen anything like that since the young Leonard Bernstein . . .' and then you read the press here, you'd think they were talking about a different person.

Anyway, that's why I admit some of my performances have been mediocre, and to a certain extent criticism was justified.

It was a lonely time for me, it has been very lonely, but it isn't any more, thank God. I've learned to take things as they come. I'm studying Asian philosophy to try and find my inner self in meditation, I go on retreat two or three times a year. All these things have helped me a lot, otherwise I think I could have broken down really . . .

The orchestra is in terrible financial difficulties at the moment, but for the first time, I'm optimistic for the orchestra, optimistic that we are artistically going the right way, optimistic in my job. The coming season is the first one I've really put my signature on, where I didn't have any problem to push it through.

I know there are people who are critical towards me, but I know the longer I stay with the orchestra, the more people I'll win over.

I now think many people in the orchestra see me as their colleague, rather than the music director.

I feel very committed to the musicians, I really want to be their friend, it goes to the extent that if there were a problem in their private life, I hope they could come to me at any time.

There are several conductors I admire. Wilhelm Furtwängler, who died in 1954, is my number one hero, I think he was the greatest in this century: how he tackles pieces, how he gets the architecture right is most amazing. I remember the first recording I heard of his was a Mozart G minor symphony. It was so exciting and so thrilling, and I subsequently bought other recordings, and got more and more into his mastery of conducting.

The second hero is Herbert von Karajan. I had the privilege of going to many of his rehearsals in his last six or seven years. He could tell exactly where a problem was and how to arrange an orchestra, he just knew everything. I also admired him for his discipline, starting with his own self-discipline, as he was a very sick man, and in real agony all the time because of his back.

My third hero is Leonard Bernstein, whose rehearsals I also went to. I liked the wild animal in Bernstein, the way he threw himself into a performance was fascinating, the energy he had and the commitment to his music were inspiring, and even if you did not agree with him stylistically, it still was exciting what he did.

Although I've gone away from the Catholic church, I'm a very religious person. I think that I'm here to serve my musical talent, I do believe, as it says in the Bible, if you have a talent you must deal with it properly, which means you have to make it grow. To have talent is a great gift, but it's also a duty, and I do know that I can give people quite a lot through it.

List of Musicians

RICHARD BISSILL
French Horn

STEVE BROOM
Viola

COLIN BUSBY
Trombone

NICHOLAS BUSCH
French Horn

TONY BYRNE
Viola

RON CALDER
Cello

SANTIAGO CARVALHO
Cello

CELIA CHAMBERS
Flute

SIMON CHANNING
Flute

CATHY CRAIG
First Violins

DERMOT CREHAN
Second Violins

DENIS CURLETT
Trumpet

MIRANDA DAVIS
Viola

GEOFFREY DOWNS
Double Bass

ROBERT DUNCAN
Viola

LAWRIE EVANS
Trumpet

RACHEL GLEDHILL
Percussion

DAVID GODSELL
Viola

JOAN GRAHAM
Cor Anglais

TINA GRUENBERG
First Violins

COLIN HARRISON
First Violins

PETER HARVEY
Trombone

FIONA HIGHAM
Second Violins

RICHARD HOSFORD
Clarinet

NICOLA HURTON
First Violins

RUSSELL JORDAN
Timpani

THE ORCHESTRA

JOHN KITCHEN
First Violins

KATHY LOYNES
First Violins

ROGER LUNN
Cello

JOSEPH MAHER
Second Violins

RACHEL MASTERS
Harp

ANNE MCINERNY
Trumpet

GARETH MOLLISON
French Horn

SARAH NEWBOLD
Piccolo

LEO PHILLIPS
First Violin

ROBERT POOL
First Violins

GEOFFREY PRICE
Second Violins

JOHN PRICE
Bassoon

MARTIN ROBERTSON
Saxophone

KEVIN RUNDELL
Double Bass

JOSEPHINE ST LEON
Viola

BRYAN SCOTT
Double Bass

JOHN SHARP
Cello

JULIAN SHAW
Viola

OWEN SLADE
Tuba

STEPHEN SMITH
Guitar

JOAKIM SVENHEDEN
Leader

ANGELA TENNICK
Oboe

STEPHEN TRIER
Clarinet

BOB TRUMAN
Cello

FRANZ WELSER-MÖST
Conductor

★   ★   ★

JOHN COBB
Personnel Manager

KEN GRAHAM
Stage Manager

JUDITH GRAHAME
Marketing Director